Not Your Mother'
On Travel

Created by
Dahlynn McKowen,
Ken McKowen and Terri Elders

Published by
Publishing Syndicate

 PO Box 607
Orangevale California 95662
www.PublishingSyndicate.com

P9-BYM-230

Not Your Mother's Book . . .
On Travel

*We would like to thank the many individuals
who granted us permission to reprint their stories.
See the complete listing beginning on page 310.*

Created and edited by Dahlynn McKowen,
Ken McKowen and Terri Elders
Cover and Book Design by Publishing Syndicate
Cover photo: Africa Studio/Shutterstock.com
Copyeditor: Dahlynn McKowen
Proofreader: Pat Nelson

Published by
Publishing Syndicate
PO Box 607
Orangevale California 95662

www.PublishingSyndicate.com
www.Facebook.com/PublishingSyndicate
Twitter: @PublishingSynd

Print Edition ISBN: 978-1-938778-04-9
EPUB Digital Edition ISBN: 978-1-938778-05-6
Library of Congress Control Number 2012921793

Printed in Canada.

This book is a collaborative effort. Writers from all over the world submitted their work for consideration, with 58 stories making the final cut. All contributors are compensated for their stories.

Publishing Syndicate strongly encourages you to submit your story for one of its many anthologies. You'll find information on how to do so at the end of this book, starting on page 312.

~~ To Kelly C. Presley ~~

1933-2008

From 1983 when we met at the Paradise Café in Long Beach, California, Kelly urged me to regard life as a feast. "Savor every moment," he'd insist. "Follow your dreams."

So we'd scamper off to Baja for lobster, Palm Springs for calamari, and Mendocino for wine tasting. Eventually we headed to Central America on a shared five-year adventure. While we feasted, we also wrote, read and plotted new destinations. We'd work our way to Uruguay, we agreed.

Then we each dreamed new dreams that led us to travel separately. But our friendship endured, fueled by our mutual admiration for Willie Nelson, the Lakers, author Charles Bukowski, herb-stuffed pork loins . . . and exotic locales.

Sweet KC, you're always on my mind. We never quite made it to Montevideo, but we did have La Antigua.

~~ Terri Elders

Kelly enjoying his garden.

Terri and Kelly

CONTENTS

4 Expect the Unexpected 109

5 Planes, Trains and Automobiles 141

6 The Great Outdoors 187

Acknowledgments

Lots of people to thank, all around the world!

From Terri:

Thank you, Phil Yeh, "the godfather of the graphic novel," who, for over three decades, has published my travel articles and literary adventures in *Uncle Jam*, the world's best free arts magazine.

Thank you, Jane Conn of Colville, Washington, for sharing my interest in literary England and joining me on "The Best of Times" Charles Dickens excursion in his 2012 bicentennial year.

And I am grateful to my son, Steve Elders, my stepsons, Scott, Rick and Darren Wilson, and my five fur kids—Tsunami, Natty, Groucho, Harpo and Chico—for allowing me to write about them whenever I have the whim to do so.

From Dahlynn and Ken:

Thank you to Dahlynn's teen son Shawn, for putting up with the general mayhem that every new book brings to the McKowen household.

Thank you, Pat Nelson, for being our proofreader extraordinaire. You R the "bestest" proofer in the "hole" world ¡¡

Thank you to all the NYMB and *OMG! My Reality!* co-creators for joining us on this wonderfully crazy publishing journey.

Most of all, thank you to those who have graciously shared their stories with us, even though we couldn't fit all of your wonderful travels into the book. We couldn't have done it without you!

Mexican Riviera

St. Louis, Missouri

Agrigento, Sicily

Introduction

"Take the adventure—heed the call, now ere the irrevocable moment passes! Tis but a banging of the door behind you, a blithesome step forward, and you are out of your old life and into the new!"
~~ Kenneth Graham, *The Wind in the Willows*

When it comes to the human urge to wander the globe, many of us find it impossible not to surrender.

Many of us travel the Earth vicariously. Those who have never thumbed through a *Fodor's* travel guide or applied for a passport may find themselves entertained by the movie classic *Casablanca*, humming along with the 1960s hit song *Leaving on a Jet Plane*, or devouring Mark Twain's famed travel chronicle *The Innocents Abroad*. Other armchair travelers are fascinated by adventures they watch on both the Internet and TV, the latter of which has showcased exotic locations around the world via award-winning shows such as *Globe Trekker, Survivor* and the *The Amazing Race*.

Then there are those of us who've been badly gnawed by that travel bug. We can't sit still. We're perpetually packing our bags and chasing new horizons. For us, travel isn't about a hundred places to cross off a been-there, done-that list—it's about never letting an opportunity slip by to see the world in a new way. We return with once-in-a-lifetime memories tucked into our hearts and to be shared with our friends and family at will. The travel devout are on constant standby, ready to indulge

the urge to gypsy the world at a moment's notice, or at least when there's a great travel deal to be had.

Journey now with our writers as they abandon preconceptions, embrace new cultures, adapt to alternative amenities, and wrangle with a medley of critters, some benevolent, some menacing, some simply red-hatted.

"I hungered for the romance of the sea, and foreign ports, and foreign smiles. I wanted to follow the prow of a ship, any ship, and sail away, perhaps to China, perhaps to Spain, perhaps to the South Sea Isles, there to do nothing all day but lie on a surf-swept beach and fling monkeys at the coconuts."
~~ Richard Halliburton, *The Royal Road to Romance*

~~ Terri Elders

CHAPTER ONE

Keep an Open Mind

Embrace new experiences . . .

Catching a Cab in NYC

by
Marlene Chism

It was our last day in New York City. My friend Julie and I stood on the corner of Fifth Avenue and 32nd Street in the pouring rain, as we watched it happen again. A New Yorker slithered into a cab that we both thought I had hailed.

"She stole our cab! How dare she jump in ahead of us! That's so rude! It's not fair!" I exclaimed.

"She's also laughing at us," Julie added in an almost melodic voice. We watched the cab speed away with nary a concern that we had waved it down first.

"That's interesting," Julie said as we watched three more cabs pass us by. Julie's calm interest in our current situation only fueled my fire.

"I'm furious," I reiterated, trying to convince her of the severity of the situation as we stood in the rain, luggage in tow, only to be passed by again and again.

Growing up in the Midwest certainly hadn't taught me or Julie how to hail a cab in New York City, and the embarrassment of feeling completely incompetent increased my aggravation as cab after cab passed by.

"If I could just figure out the rules of getting a cab in New York City, we'd be out of the rain and on the way to the airport," I said, probably more to myself than to Julie.

"I believe I read somewhere that there are certain rules about hailing a cab," I continued, louder this time. "Does a bright light mean he is on duty or off duty? Does it mean he already has a passenger or is he looking for a passenger? What does it take to get a cab?" Apparently Julie thought these were rhetorical questions because she didn't deign to answer.

So far, I had learned several things that didn't work. Standing timidly on the corner and waving like a 5-year-old who just saw Santa only got me a few friendly waves from cab drivers with passengers already aboard. Apparently nobody either noticed or appreciated my politeness. And waiting my turn didn't seem to register with the street-savvy New Yorkers who don't believe in a first-come, first-served basis, but operated instead on the every-man-for-himself philosophy.

"Do you think there's a best time of day to hail a cab, or a certain way to stand to get their attention?" I asked Julie, who seemed to be growing tired of my inquisitiveness.

"I'll just walk back to the hotel and give the concierge five bucks to help us hail a cab," Julie said, with a sigh of resignation. The thought of wasting five dollars to do something as simple as hailing a cab was something I simply could not allow.

"Absolutely not!" I screamed. "Five dollars buys a large

Dairy Queen choco-covered strawberry Blizzard! I'm going to hail a cab if it's the last thing I ever do in New York City!"

"OK then, but don't be angry," Julie said. "Let's look at this experience as a way to quit resisting 'what is' and a chance to watch other people so we can learn what to do."

"I don't want to learn. I just want a cab to pick us up and get us out of this nasty rain!" I shouted over the traffic noise.

In my fury, I boldly stepped off the curb and stuck my hand out, as if I were hailing Hitler and voila! A cab appeared instantaneously to pick us up.

"Now, that's more like it," I exclaimed, feeling a surge of power.

"LaGuardia Airport," I said to the cab driver, as I winked smugly at Julie. I surmised that Julie was glad she still had her five dollars and now was quite impressed with my newfound cab-hailing abilities.

The dead-eyed cab driver's expression gave no indication of what he thought about taking us to the airport. I decided to find out for myself.

"Did I just ruin your day? I mean, when you go to the cab driver's convention, do they tell jokes about someone from the Midwest hailing a cab and then when you find out they are going to LaGuardia, does everyone moan and laugh at the punch line when you say you wish you had hung yourself instead?" I asked him.

"No, I'm glad you are going to the airport. It's more money for me," he said, in a thick Polish accent.

"Well, I couldn't tell by the tone of your voice," I said, straining to see his expression, and trying to sound cheerful.

"That's a good thing, to take someone to LaGuardia on a very busy Sunday," he said, without cracking a smile.

"Then you should smile. This is your lucky day," I continued. Now that I had accomplished my first goal of hailing a cab, my new goal was getting the cab driver to chat.

"So, what are the rules of hailing a cab? When your light is on, does that mean you are on duty, empty, full, or is that just for decoration? I keep trying to figure it out, but I still don't really understand."

Without taking a breath or a moment to ponder, he replied, "You don't need to figure out anything. There are over 12,000 cabs in New York, and we are all looking for you. Just raise your hand."

Hmmmm. I pondered all of the life lessons in this experience. Life isn't always fair: sometimes people will steal your cab and laugh at you while they're doing it. Anger isn't always a bad thing: sometimes it can help you to get out of the rain. Some people never smile, even when they are happy, but you can always learn something from everyone. You don't always have to figure it out, but you do have to raise your hand and ask for what you want. If the answer is no, or you miss your chance, there are 12,000 other chances around the corner.

Finally, you can always pay someone to help you with things you don't know, but sometimes it's better to save the $5 for a Dairy Queen choco-covered strawberry Blizzard.

Sunny Side Up in Panzano

by

Risa Nye

When it comes to travel, I'm a late bloomer. I didn't go backpacking around Europe during my teens and twenties. No youth hostels, no scary adventures on trains, no one-night stands with handsome strangers, no emergency phone calls home when money ran out. Instead, I got a full-time job at 18, worked my way through college and got married at 21.

Truthfully, I was a homebody and immune to the wanderlust that infected my contemporaries. I didn't begrudge them their Eurail passes and souvenirs. I just figured that someday I'd get over my reluctance—or, to be honest, my anxiety—about traveling, and when that happened, I'd get on a plane or a train and go somewhere. And when it did finally happen, I was nearly 50 years old. Travel at that age—minus backpacks, youth hostels and begging parents to wire cash—promised to be a different sort of adventure.

My first trip to Europe proved a perfect introduction to travel for a novice like me. I went to Paris on a tour organized by fashion and design experts. Our lodging and most of our meals were pre-arranged by our guides who knew the city inside and out. We visited many of the places a first-time tourist would expect to see, but we also got to go where most visitors can't.

We were given behind-the-scenes tours of the opera's costume shops, where a tailor, bent over a large cutting table, chalked the outlines of a suit, and a seamstress let us touch the fine pleats on a satin bodice. We peeked into a room where a proud staff member meticulously pressed delicate ruffled collars and cuffs. We visited a small family-owned business that produced hand-sewn fabric flowers.

One afternoon I set out on my own and got lost, and then soaked in a sudden downpour. With the help of a young *gendarme*, I found my way back to the hotel, proud I'd been drenched in Paris rain. I had a good story to tell at dinner that night, and by the time our tour ended on a gray, drizzly Bastille Day, I knew I'd overcome my travel phobia.

The following year, my friend Chris asked me to join her and another friend on a walking trip through Tuscany. I accepted. For weeks we prepared by walking uphill around our neighborhood, toting heavy cans of soup in our daypacks. Finally we felt ready.

The three of us, middle-aged women sans our husbands, joined an international group of energetic walkers on an Italian journey that would begin in Siena and end in Montepulciano. No leisurely stroll through the vineyards, as the schedule showed that we would be walking eight to 10 miles a day—

which we did—during one of the hottest Junes in Italy's history. At the end of each day we felt bone weary and our feet ached, but we'd refresh with a shower and a feet-up rest in our rooms, followed by a lukewarm gin-and-tonic at the closest bar.

We conquered hills along the Strada Blanca and traipsed through miles of nodding sunflowers and fields of bundled hay. The company of new friends—along with the promise of plenty of good food and wine every evening, in addition to our daily dose of gelato—kept our feet moving and our spirits high, despite the oppressive heat.

When the walking tour ended, the three of us set off to explore nearby towns in Chianti. In a converted villa in the tiny town of Panzano, I experienced my most unusual adventure, at the hands of a dark-haired woman named Stefania.

While we checked into our carnation-pink villa, I noticed an advertisement in the lobby for spa treatments. I nudged my friends and said, "Let's do it!" My companions agreed. They eagerly signed up for hand and foot massages or facials, but I opted for a full-hour body massage with the masseuse, Stefania. My legs ached, my feet ached and I longed for that familiar dreamy half-sleep after a good hour of kneading.

I settled into my airy blue room, relaxed, wrote in my journal, and waited for the appointed hour to arrive. Soon Stefania knocked gently at my door, and softly announced herself. She fussed over the bed, spreading out a sheet and a towel, and then motioned for me to lie face down and cover up with the towel. Her English and my Italian met somewhere in the middle. Words didn't seem to be necessary. I knew what I was supposed to do next. She stepped outside while I undressed.

I judged her to be professional but friendly, and I hoped her hands were soft and smooth. I slipped under the towel, on top of the cool white sheet, and closed my eyes. I was so sore and tired that the mere thought of someone working my muscles filled me with relief and joy.

Stefania returned after a few moments and began kneading my back, shoulders and legs—deftly folding the towel over and back, up one side and down the other. I was sinking into that familiar state of relaxation, inhaling the scented oil and listening to the buzz and hum of nature outside my window. When she finished my back, Stefania tapped me on the shoulder and motioned for me to roll over. In the next instant, she flipped down the towel.

There I was, naked from the waist up, not entirely sure whether this was local custom or something else. *Well, now what?* I thought.

Stefania continued the massage, working her well-oiled hands in large circles from my shoulders down to my waist. There's no getting around the fact that this was, in fact, a breast massage. After my initial startled reaction to the surprise unveiling, I began breathing normally and enjoyed the sensation of her capable hands as they moved rhythmically up and down my torso. I found it pleasurable, but not in an erotic sense; Stefania was all business. *This must be the way things are done here*, I thought. *No turning back now*. So I focused on the ceiling fan as it spun in a lazy circle, thinking about how I would describe this feeling to my friends. *Nice*, I decided. *Very nice.*

When she finished, Stefania slipped quietly out of the room. I dozed off, relaxed and content.

Early that evening, I met my friends by the little pool behind the inn. "How were your massages?" I asked.

"Fine," they said. "And how was yours?"

So I told them—everything. After a moment of stunned silence, we all burst out laughing. For the rest of the trip, any time we saw two hills together—or two of anything together, really—I got a gentle poke in the ribs and a wink from my companions.

I still wonder—did Stefania follow standard European massage procedures, or did I get the Stefania Special? I'll never know, and I don't really care.

My first trip to Italy had been filled with surprising pleasures and unexpected beauty. My favorite memories are of the seas of yellow Tuscan sunflowers, the welcome taste of cold gelato on a hot day, and my time with Stefania, sunny side up in Panzano.

Risa in Panzano

Craving Creature Comforts

by
Terri Elders

"What do you miss the most?"

I'd lived in developing countries for a decade, so was used to this question from friends and relatives.

"Creature comforts," I'd always reply. "Just the usual take-for-granted things I enjoyed all the time in Southern California... the Lakers on TV, hot bubble baths, Sunday papers with book and movie reviews, and frozen yogurt."

What I didn't confess was that I also missed my boyfriend's hugs.

The weeks leading up to my 57th birthday had been devoid of much comfort at all. A Peace Corps Volunteer, I served in the Dominican Republic, not far from the Haitian border. Recently I'd struggled with a recurring festering heat rash, resistant to calamine lotion or talcum powder. I'd also suffered sleep deprivation since my neighbor, Julio, had switched to swing shift and now relaxed after work by booming *merengue* music at midnight. Most discomforting of all, I'd been blind-sided by a letter from my longtime on-and-off-again boy-friend. He'd written that, out of the blue, he'd met someone he figured was the love of his life and married her.

In shock, I realized I'd have to do without those hugs permanently. I supposed I'd miss them more than hot bubble baths or even sleep. I wallowed in grief for days, and then woke up one morning and realized it was my birthday. I decided I'd pamper myself. I couldn't undo the past and had no control over the future, but I could treat myself to something com-forting this very day. I debated whether I'd stop after work for a Presidente, which was the good local brew, at my favorite fried chicken café, or if I'd reward myself with a chocolate chip waffle cone at Helados Bon.

I mulled it over late that afternoon in my nook at the back of Social Services of Dominican Churches where I was assembling collages for the volunteer preschools in the *campos* surrounding the town. Usually in June, the temperature and humidity in San Juan de la Maguana both pushed 95. I prayed my heat rash wouldn't make a comeback, as I swabbed my red bandana across my forehead. Careful that I wouldn't drip on my pastiche, I'd scissor out a tiger or a cow from my stack of old magazines, slap some rubber cement on the creature's back and press it into place on a sheet of cardboard. This one, *Ani-males*, nearly was finished . . . and so was I for the day.

Time to decide. Helados Bon made the best chocolate chip ice cream, not only in the town of San Juan de la Ma-guana, but in the entire world. My mouth began to water just thinking about that first lick. *They really should call it chunk, not chip,* I thought, blotting my forehead for the fifth time in the last five minutes. The slivers of dark chocolate that studded the creamy vanilla ice cream were the size of my thumbnail.

I affixed a final cutout fox to the upper left hand corner of my cardboard, patted the curling edge of an elephant's trunk back into place, and set *Animales* down next to *Vegetales* to dry overnight. Tomorrow I'd assemble *Minerales* and coat the trio with shellac. In the mid 1990s we didn't have lamination in the western D.R.

In fact, we didn't have a lot of things that I'd appreciate having, especially on my birthday, I grumped. Back home I used to treat myself to a candlelight bubble bath on my special day. Here, of course, I lacked both a tub and hot water from the tap. I took cold showers when there was running water and bucket baths from a barrel when there wasn't.

Oh, oh, I warned myself. *Stop dwelling on what you don't have . . . think about what you do. And that's ice cream!*

I headed out the door. As I strolled past the street vendors who crowded every downtown corner, I ignored their shouts of, "Helados, helados!" Sure, I could settle for one of their plastic-covered tube ice creams, but this was my special day. I didn't mind walking the eight blocks to Helados Bon, even at the risk of reactivating that pesky rash.

Once I reached the shop, I stood in line for 15 minutes or more, amusing myself by watching Dominicans, many cuddling babies, as they swayed to the frantic beat of merengue. Always hugging, always dancing, always upbeat. *I wished I could emulate them,* I thought, inching forward in the queue.

When I got up to the counter I noticed that chocolate chip was not listed on the blackboard that carried the day's flavors. Only chocolate, vanilla, *bizcocho* (cake), and *chinola* (passion fruit) appeared to be on offer.

"No chocolate chip?" I asked, pronouncing it the Dominican way—*choc-o-latte cheep*.

"No." The counter girl shook her head sadly to indicate how sorry she was. "Bizcocho? Chinola?"

I hesitated. I didn't want cake, even if it were my birthday, and I'd just said goodbye to passion, so didn't need any frozen reminders of my current loveless, hugless circumstances. I settled for my second choice and walked over to Pica Pollo for an icy Presidente and *tostones*, which were the fried plantains that outsold french fries in the D.R. I slid onto the bench of one of the patio picnic tables, plunked down my tray and dipped a tostone into a little paper cup of catsup.

"Buen provecho," somebody said. I turned to see who was encouraging me to enjoy my snack. It was Julio, my boombox-loving neighbor, and he had just planted his tray beside mine. I couldn't believe my luck. I searched my meager Spanish vocabulary for just the right words.

"No puedo dormir en la noche," I began, hoping he'd understand why I haven't been able to sleep at night.

Julio's hand flew to his heart.

"¡No!" he exclaimed, "Es mi música."

I nodded. Yes, it was his music.

He yanked my sodden kerchief from my left hand and squeezed my fingers as he apologized. Never again, he swore. We nodded, nibbled and nattered. Julio did most of the nattering, since my Spanish, even after two years, remained pretty basic. When he left to go to work, Julio hugged me. Not the hug I'd been missing... nonetheless, a hug.

That night as I readied myself for bed, I took inventory. No bubble baths, television or frozen yogurt. Not even Helados Bon. But it had been a pretty good day. I'd finished *Animales*, my creature collage. I hadn't cried over my feckless ex or even over an ice cream flavor that wasn't available. I hadn't suffered another outbreak of prickly heat. I'd even extracted a promise from Julio for a good night's sleep.

I realized I'd managed to stay in the present, rather than sniveling about the past or fretting over the future. I'd simply accepted what niceties had come my way. There'd be plenty of time in the future for the Lakers on TV and Sunday papers, for bubble baths and frozen yogurt, and perhaps to find another boyfriend to provide an occasional hug.

I closed my eyes, grinning in the silence. Someday I might even tell curious friends that what I miss the most are... merengue and tostones.

Fellow Peace Corps Volunteer Pat Gray and Terri (in skirt) dancing the merengue, Dominican Republic, 1994

Half Right

by

Sioux Roslawski

"You know, don't you, that in France the women go topless on the beach—and your mom will be topless, too!" My husband's voice was approaching a girlish shriek, moving close to a pitch that only dogs could hear—so filled with glee was he. Michael was up to no good.

My son's eyes widened to the size of small saucers. His face visibly paled, and I think I spotted a few beads of sweat popping up on his forehead. He was 14 and any part of his mother's naked body was the last thing he wanted to see.

My husband, a homebody, had no interest in traveling to Europe, and was trying to use scare tactics to take the shine off France's allure. But alas, it was all in vain. I was already in love with all things French—this would be my second trip there—and our boy was eager to travel to a foreign country.

I assured Ian that his mother would definitely not be topless on any beach, and I then shot a scathing look at Michael. With my eyes working in concert with my eyebrows, I silently asked: *Does he want to lose a body part? Does he feel lucky? Because he's not going to get "lucky" anytime soon if he keeps this up.* But apparently a couple of decades with me had thickened Michael's skin, enabling him to ignore my burning stink-eye, because he continued.

"And Speedos. When you're in France, you'll have to wear a Speedo." This caused almost as much emotional distress for Ian as the thought of his mother semi-nude. As a gangly teenager, Ian's swimwear consisted of a pair of baggy, boxy swim trunks. So much heavy cotton encased him, it was impossible to tell he was rail-thin. The idea of wearing skintight, form-fitting, shape-showing spandex on the beach? The thought made him blanch once more.

Again, I reassured Ian there was no Speedo law in France. He would not be put into a French prison if he refused to succumb to the charms of the skintight swimsuit. Although every photo I saw of French beaches did perplex me. Like my husband, I couldn't understand the fascination. All the men—no matter what shape they were in or what age they were—wore a Speedo. *What was with that?* I pondered. However, I was sure there was no way my son would be tied down and forced to wear a spandex swimsuit. The land of croissants and brie would embrace my boy with his baggy beachwear. Of that I was sure.

Secure in the knowledge that he would *not* see his mother topless and he would *not* have to wear a Speedo, my son said goodbye to his dad and eagerly boarded the plane with me. I spent the in-flight hours reading and daydreaming of all the things we were going to do and see. My son napped and played video games.

Once we landed in Toulouse, Virginie—who had been my "sister" for the year she was in the U.S. as a foreign exchange student—and her family picked us up, and we drove to their home in the country. Settling in, we savored the slow pace of rural France. We had leisurely outdoor breakfasts of bread and tea. We spent a weekend surrounded by the Pyrenees and swam in an icy lake, the waters cascading straight down from the craggy mountains. Our dinners routinely stretched for three or four hours, full of conversation and laughter, and we relished every mouthful.

It was two weeks we would never forget. A mother-and-son bond became stronger, cemented by experiencing together different foods, a different language and different landscapes. The charm of the country lured my son to return a few years later, so enamored he was with France. But what about that promise about Ian's mom keeping her top on and Ian avoiding a Speedo? I was only half right.

We immediately discovered that many of the women who went topless should have rethought their decision. French women were floppy, just like me, and Virginie and I both kept our heads *and* our tops on. And for that, I have the eternal thanks of an entire nation.

The Speedo, however, was unavoidable. One afternoon at a French waterpark, my son met his Waterloo. Men and boys must wear Speedo-style swimsuits, according to the park's rules. Ian's surfer-boy canvas swimwear that went almost to his knees obviously was against the regulations. We were unprepared and brainstormed various alternatives, including him just wearing his underwear. We were flummoxed until Virginie and I went to the front desk and tried to plead our case. We were from another country. It was the only suit he had. Couldn't they make an exception?

No, but for a nominal fee they could rent us a Speedo.

So that hot afternoon, I was proved wrong. Ian was forced to wear a Speedo. But I'd been right in assuming the prospect of wearing a used skintight suit, where other guys' junk had once been, would be beyond repugnant to my boy. So I lied.

"Ian, they had some swimsuits for sale. We bought one for you. Hurry up and put it on so we can go in."

Later, as we were loading up the car with our towels and our picnic basket, one of us grabbed the Speedo out of the bag and stealthily returned it to the front desk.

Mama may not always be right, but Mama does know best.

Find the guy on the French beach wearing a Speedo!

Always Look a Tiger in the Eye

by
SuzAnne C. Cole

We were only a 10-minute walk from the security of Tiger Tops Tented Camp in Nepal, led by our guide, the camp manager known simply as "B.C." He had earned this nickname because his real name was unpronounceable by us thick-tongued Americans.

B.C. stopped and signaled us to gather around him. *Why were we stopping already? Did he think we were wimps?* I thought to myself. The four of us, the only tourists in the camp at that time, were considerably overdressed compared with B.C., who wore a T-shirt, dress slacks and flimsy canvas shoes. We, on the other hand, had on sturdy gear and high boots and carried walking sticks. After a week of hiking in the Annapurnas—a section of the Himalayas in north-central Nepal—we four felt fit and confident.

"I need to give you a safety lecture," B.C. explained.

Safety lecture? For a hike that was presented as a pleasant way to spend a morning, a stroll up to a ridge to view the river boundaries of the camp and to bird-watch? B.C., like all the guides in the camp, didn't even carry a rifle. Only the soldiers stationed at the entrance to the camp to guard against a potential guerilla attack were armed. I glanced at Prem, our trip guide, but he looked as impassive as the former Gurkha he was. Earlier in the trip, he'd described his British army training, when he'd seen soldiers staked naked on anthills for poor performance on the shooting range. He had no need of a safety lecture from anyone.

"If we run into rhinos," B.C. declared, "here is what you will do." *Run into rhinos? I wouldn't even walk into one.* The day before, I'd viewed some from the back of a friendly elephant on an early morning game ride—that was as close as I ever intended to get.

"If there's a big tree nearby, get behind it."

What if another hiker has already beat you to it? I eyed the other three—Joe, Mary and my husband—and mentally rated my chances of winning a hand-to-hand struggle with any of them. *Dead last.*

"If there is time, climb the big tree." *Have I ever even climbed a single tree?* I thought, recalling having done so once. But it was a tree with ladder steps nailed to its trunk. Mostly I'd misspent my youth reading.

"If there are no big trees nearby, crawl under a bush." Visualizing myself on hands and knees scrambling under a bush, rear end an exposed target, I choked back a hysterical laugh.

"Now that is what to do for rhinos. Sloth bears are different."

Sloth bears? What the hell is that? Sloths, yes, ambling upside down on a tree limb high above me in the rain forests of Costa Rica, were no problem. Even I could run faster than that. And once I'd seen a bear while hiking, but through binoculars, as it rambled across the far side of a valley.

"For the sloth bear, we gather into a tight circle, clap our hands and shout." I resisted the impulse to ask if he'd brought music.

"Now for tigers, it is important to look them in the eye." *Tigers?!* True, the camp was called Tiger Tops. And I wanted to see one. But only from the back of my elephant friend as she, not me, eyeballed the striped beast.

"While maintaining eye contact, back slowly away. Do not run." Every survival gene I had in my body was screaming, *Run, run, run! Don't stop until you're on a plane heading back to Texas!*

As we silently digested this lecture, I waited for someone to ask the obvious question. But no one did.

"So, B.C.," I squeaked as casually as possible through a throat which seemed to have squeezed shut. "How often have your hiking groups had to use this excellent information?"

"Oh," he responded, "not for a long time. The last rhino was five or six . . . (*Years,* I thought. *Good, good.*) . . . months ago."

About sightings of sloth bears and tigers, he was silent and I did not have the heart to ask.

"Only the next 20 minutes of our hike is on flat land. Once we start climbing to the ridge, we are safe from the rhinos. They do not like to climb."

Neither do I, particularly, but that day I hiked as briskly toward that climb as possible. OK, call it a jog, as though climbing were my favorite sport in the entire world. Prem tried to hide a grin. No doubt he was remembering my snail-slow progress up the last 400 stone steps to Ghandruk, a village in the Annapurnas. At that time, I didn't think I could manage another step even after he'd promised hot water and cold beer. His implicit threat was our having to eat and sleep on the floor of a dirty teahouse, perhaps the one called The Tasty Tongue, if I didn't pick up my pace a little. He was probably wishing he'd had a tiger to hasten my steps that day.

As it happened, we did not need the safety instructions. We climbed and appreciated the views—as well as I could while constantly looking over my shoulder. However, we met nothing more bothersome than rain—most unusual, as we'd been told it never rained after the monsoons.

We left Tiger Tops on the third day, walked to the river, crossed via a footbridge, and then climbed into Jeeps that took us through the forest to another river. Here we crossed in dugout canoes, and then had one final Jeep ride to the grass airstrip where women dried their laundry and grazed their goats and water buffalo. Whenever the siren signaled the approach of a plane, the livestock were herded off the runway and the laundry hastily gathered. On that day, we watched as a Yeti Airlines plane landed, and as Tiger Tops' newest guests—a couple from Dallas—emerged.

Passing the couple on our way to board, the gal asked, "How was it?" I glanced at the newcomers' crisp white shirts, creased khakis, heavy gold jewelry, good leather loafers and finally at her bouffant hairdo.

"Great," I said, "as long as you remember to always look a tiger in the eye."

Top: Hikers enjoying an elephant ride at Tiger Tops Jungle Lodge.

Bottom: Gurung Lodge in the Annapurnas

The Dark Side of the City of Light

by
Gia Sola

The Bois de Boulogne is a remnant of a prehistoric forest once used by the kings of France as a hunting ground. This park on the western flank of Paris offers a portrait of tranquility in the midst of the city, with its meandering pathways, spectacular flower displays, boating and bike rentals. It's an unlikely locale for unseemly connections, such as voyeurs—or exhibitionists.

But under the cover of darkness, the Bois puts on a different persona. Take a nighttime ride through these ancient woods and you'll find it's still a hunting ground—a human hunting ground—and not a place for the uninitiated, or at least, not for the uninformed. So if you dare to drive through this majestic preserve, be sure to lock your car doors.

We were an American threesome and one Parisian businessman and had just concluded a four-course meal taken in the French tradition. That is, accompanied by five bottles of wine. I traveled with Noel and Clarisse. It was my first trip to France.

Yves had joined us during our weekend sojourn in Paris, sharing his city like a tour guide, from the Montmartre to the Eiffel Tower, where the clock was counting down to the year 2000. On our final night he'd suggested a tour not found in the guidebooks, and we embarked on a ride along the edge of the Bois, on the edge of the second millennium.

"Take off your blouse," Yves whispered in a voice rough from Galois cigarettes, "if you want to see the show." His irreverent request sounded somehow respectful. His hooded eyes, generally relaxed in a noncommittal, albeit disdainful, expression, were narrowed and taut, revealing an intensity I hadn't seen before, a facet of the French personality I found intriguing.

He'd addressed Clarisse, his former love, who sat in the Citroën's backseat beside her new husband, the silver-haired Noel, a native New Yorker who, 10 years earlier, had been married to me. We'd had a reunion of sorts, and were comfortably familiar with the arrangement. Now all the champagne we'd consumed during dinner made us giddy as we rode through the park in the dark.

Noel laughed, repeating Yves' suggestive suggestion. "Go on, babe, go on. Show 'em your French 38s," he chanted to Clarisse. "Let's lure the depravity out of the woods."

"I'm not sure it's good to be so bold," she said.

"It's not bad to be bold," Noel countered. "It's simply a chance for some exotic fun."

"Just for fun, you say? Well, OK. Ooh la la." Clarisse sang, dropping her reservations to pull her shirt off over her head. With more of our enthusiastic encouragement, she hiked up her skirt and shimmied her shoulders like a cheerleader. It's as if she was rousing us up for a sporting event. And soon, we were all tittering right along with her.

We know they're out there, the boys of the Bois. Yves had warned us what to expect. Yet we were unprepared when suddenly we found ourselves returning the stares of three Parisian perverts peering wide-eyed into our car window. Then another arrived. Soon a dozen or more encircled our car. Young and old, black and white, fresh-faced and clean-cut, they wore blue jeans and T-shirts, well-tailored suits, even ties.

Before long, our quartet wore coats of perspiration with big beads of sweat covering each of our brows. The air in the car took on an acrid smell—the odor of fear. Outside, the bucolic view was obscured as the car was engulfed by the horde, approaching like zombies gliding out from the cover of the primeval forest.

And then, as I heaved an astonished breath, the white pearl buttons on the bodice of my black lace dress undid themselves.

* * *

For 200 years, the local populace has tolerated disreputable displays in the dark corners of this 17-acre park. In 1814, with Napoleon exiled on the Island of Elba and Paris filled with demobilized soldiers, the Bois de Boulogne was a vast encampment that the curious visited as if it were theater. And neither its annexation to the city in 1860 nor its severance—caused by the opening of the circular railway around Paris—had any effect on the games people played.

This section of the Bois is no less a theater today, with dramatic performances nightly. Cars glide through the wooded stage, their lascivious occupants coming to see and be seen. And just as in days past, there was an implicit agreement of tolerance, with an office of the commissariat and a four-story foreign embassy building situated near the boundary of it all. So, too, the street straddling the park offered a preposterous production with an array of transvestites arrrayed in all their glory, tripping along in swishing satin evening gowns and stiletto heels that clacked against the sidewalk in a crude melody. Others strutted their stuff in lingerie and painted faces, muscles and G-strings bulging. "Bisous," they cooed. Who wants kisses?

Yves asked for a kiss from me. He'd whispered his request after dinner, before we'd made this detour back to the heart of the City of Light. I'd pursed my lips around a gentle refusal, which he'd accepted like a gentleman as we cruised past the illuminated Palace of Versailles. "A tutorial, then," he'd said. "Did you know the living conditions during the reign of Louis XIV were so *honteux*, so disgraceful, that contemporary accounts described the Palace as an 'unacceptable state of unhygienic squalor'?"

I hadn't known that. But by the climax of our vicarious tour, it felt as if we were in a state of squalid adulteration ourselves. Or maybe I should call it moral debasement.

* * *

"Lock the doors," Yves had warned after we'd left the strutting strumpets behind and turned onto the narrow road that snaked its way through the Bois. A commuter route by day, at night the traffic is of the human kind. And the locals have a name for it—

La Rue Des Branleurs, The Street of the Masturbators.

We'd found the aberrant admirers lurking in the dark, in among the trees, awaiting the parade of creepers and peepers.

"Look at the way they're homing in on us!" Noel exclaimed.

Like bees to a hive, they swarmed us, but my ears were buzzing too loud to hear them. Instead, I paid mute witness. My companions were watching too, while the assemblage jostled for position, virtually swallowing up the vehicle and trapping us inside.

My fear only arose after I'd exposed my breasts. Now I tried to fill my buttonholes again, tried to catch my breath. In and out, in and out, in and out, I breathed as the surreal throng continued to emerge from the forest. A captured audience, our collective breath steamed up the tempered glass, yet we could clearly see each man press his face against the window, his hand against his manhood.

When Yves pressed me for a kiss, I didn't resist. However, this taste of the dark side left my mouth bitter, as the momentum of the mob outside the car gave rise to alarm within. But before I could voice my growing panic, I was silenced by the intruding glare of flashlights. Like the strobes of a disco, pulsating beams illuminated the car's interior, casting their garish light on our exposed flesh, dancing around Clarisse's long bare legs.

"Keep them closed," Yves cautioned, "or they'll try to break the windows."

We didn't dare get near the windows. By now we could barely see out of them. And if we could see, what we would see likely wouldn't be faces.

When the car began to rock under the weight of the bodies climbing over it, Yves said it was time to bid the Bois adieu. He looked at me—"Faire bien?" he asked—then he keyed the ignition, and the car lurched into gear.

"I'm OK," I said, still fumbling with the buttons on my dress. When he looked at me again, his furrowed brow and flared nostrils had taken on the guise of a gargoyle in the shadowy light. It was a comic effect in the midst of the drama.

Two of the tenacious bucks from the Bois were hanging onto the hood and nervous giggles pierced the atmosphere as Yves rotated the wheel to and fro in a Hollywood maneuver designed to shake off the precariously poised boys. "Au revoir," he hissed.

The heady laughter left us once we reached the center of Paris. We were all spent. It was after midnight when Yves dropped us at the hotel, a 16th-century mansion in the district called *Le Marais*. We roused the sleeping desk clerk and then climbed the marble stairway to rooms overlooking a street busy with all-night traffic.

But the sound of honking motor scooters racing under the window wasn't what kept me awake on my last night in Paris. It was that nightmare dream of my ride on the dark side.

In Search of Satisfaction

by
Ken McKowen

In 1969, I had been stationed at a special intelligence post on Japan's southern island of Kyushu for about a year when I decided to volunteer for Vietnam. The Army was quick to OK my request, and for the next 19 months I found myself touring the mountains, jungles, villages and larger cities of South Vietnam's northern provinces. Initially Phu Bai, then nearby Camp Eagle, home of the 101st Airborne Division, became my home base. From there I spent most of my days and nights leading three- and four-man special intelligence teams to mountaintop fire support bases.

I returned to Vietnam nearly 40 years later as a tourist. Vietnam was—and remains—a beautiful country with beautiful people. This time, all my shooting was done with a camera instead of an M-16. And I had the added bonus on this trip of being accompanied by three beautiful women: my wife, Dahlynn, and good friends Kathy and Teresa.

We landed in Saigon, a city the Communist government insists on calling Ho Chi Minh City, although few people who live there today abide by the government's name preference. After getting to our hotel rooms and freshening up following 20 or so hours in the air, we met for dinner. This was when we first discovered that Teresa had a major issue. She'd forgotten her hairbrush! Easy fix, right? After dinner we'd simply visit one of the many hotel gifts shops and buy her a new hairbrush. We wandered into the first shop and looked around. Lots of combs, but not a hairbrush to be found. On to another shop—same result.

Walking the streets of Saigon was a special experience. We quickly discovered that traffic signs and traffic laws were merely suggested behaviors for the drivers of the thousands of motor scooters that zipped up and down the streets. Most stopped at red lights, but nothing was guaranteed, especially if an adjacent sidewalk was available.

We roamed among the shops that filled the bottom floors of hundreds of narrow, multi-story homes crushed together along the narrow streets. Capitalism was alive and well in this peaceful communist country. But all this nonstop hustle and bustle of motorbike traffic required an act of life-threatening courage in order to cross a street, even in a painted crosswalk. Look forward, walk straight and steady, and simply let the hundreds of passing motor scooters weave around you. These mostly young-yet-experienced motor scooter pilots, often with two or more passengers or even their entire families onboard riding in front and behind them, anticipated where you would be and timed their passing to miss you. If you suddenly sped up or slowed your pace in mid-street, you'd likely get hit!

While our team didn't spend a great amount of time looking for Teresa's new hairbrush, it was never far from our minds. After several days of visiting museums and Buddhist temples, Catholic churches, old battle sites, including crawling through reconstructed underground tunnels, we traveled north to the ancient city of Hue. We hired a small and leaky wooden pram to ferry us across the city's Perfume River to one of the major public markets. We found great food, unknown items said to be food, and just about anything else one might need, from fresh fish to television sets, available for the right price, which was always negotiable. We even stopped in a small beauty salon and asked about a hairbrush. The owner showed us numerous combs and finally, a single hairbrush! Unfortunately it was used and had likely been around her shop since the war. So Teresa continued the journey hairbrush-less.

We toured Hue's great Citadel, site of a major military battle during what became known as the 1968 Tet Offensive. Filled with beautiful temples and peaceful monks, the ancient structures had been repaired and rebuilt, its great walls now with open gates that welcomed visitors.

One day we took a bus ride south along Highway One to the city of Da Nang. It had once been a huge U.S. military base, which to visit from Camp Eagle required a harrowing drive along the narrow and winding ambush alley that ran through many miles of rice paddies and mountainous jungle. We stopped at a huge statue of Buddha, visible for miles around. It had been under construction during the time I had served in Vietnam and first visited Da Nang. We found more shops, ate great food, but couldn't find a hairbrush. Teresa was not happy having to get a comb through her thick, black Sicilian hair.

After several more days we headed farther north to the country's capital of Hanoi. We toured the infamous Hanoi Hilton, where U.S. prisoners of war were held. This is the same place Senator John McCain was imprisoned after his fighter jet crashed in a nearby lake. We visited the mausoleum of North Vietnam's war hero Ho Chi Minh. Leaving the bustling city streets, we ventured to the rural coast for a boat cruise on spectacular Ha Long Bay.

On our next-to-last day in Vietnam, while Teresa stayed in her hotel room and napped, Dahlynn, Kathy and I went shopping in Hanoi's famed three-story Trang Thien Plaza. The plaza was a giant flea market with individual vendors renting spaces inside the modern complex and selling everything from clothes to jewelry to furniture. It housed a unique blend of items, ranging from international brand-named perfumes and jewelry to inexpensive knock-offs of almost everything imaginable. And here is where we found it. At one vendor's space, stacked 10-feet high with boxed and unboxed merchandise, the owner showed us a hairbrush—a brand new, never-been-used hairbrush. She insisted on giving us a hairbrush demonstration, which we felt was unnecessary—until she flipped a switch on the brush and its long, cylindrical handle began vibrating. Wow! A hairbrush and a sex toy, all in one. We didn't even dicker over the price.

We returned to the hotel, and since it was Teresa's birthday, we hurried to her room and presented the gift. She was absolutely delighted. When we flipped the small on-off switch to "on" and described the additional use for the brush, Teresa at first was perplexed and then embarrassed, while the three of us roared with laughter. That evening when we gathered for our going-home party in the hotel's restaurant, we asked Teresa how her hairbrush had worked. She turned beet red—but her hair looked great.

Top: Kathy, Teresa, Dahlynn and Ken on China Beach
Btm left: Vietnam street, 2008; Btm right: Vietnam street, 1969

CHAPTER TWO

Just the Two of Us

Our best trips are when it's
two for the road.

The Island of Bones— But Not Mine

by

Ernie Witham

I guess you could say my wife and I are well-seasoned travelers, because we always make an effort to capture the flavor of each exotic new location and its most famous inhabitants.

"Can I help you?" the tan young woman asked.

"Yes. I'd like the Ernest Hemingway fish sandwich."

"Of course. Do you want the Harry Truman fries with that or the Jimmy Buffet soup?"

Thus began another day of historic proportions in *Cayo Hueso* or Island of Bones, better known as Key West, Florida. Key West, a mysterious island community filled with artists, writers, musicians and other people who drink a lot, is the southernmost point in the continental United States, as is illustrated by signs at the end of Duval Street indicating the southernmost house, the southernmost hotel, and Bob, the southernmost panhandler.

It was a Wednesday in late June, and the temperature outside our bodies was about the same as the temperature inside our bodies. Still, we were not there to lie around by a shaded pool all day. What kind of a vacation would that be?

"What's next on the itinerary?" my wife asked.

"Well, we haven't seen the world's largest turtle shell yet or the place the islanders used to hold the cock fights. Says here it's now a KFC."

"Naw. I want to do something adventurous today," my wife said.

I felt a little twinge. Last time she said that we ended up six miles out in the Atlantic Ocean at the coral reef.

"Here we are," the captain had informed us on that fateful day, after a 45-minute boat ride that reduced the land behind us to a mere memory. "Snorkel up. And be careful of your footing. We've had more accidents this summer from people slipping than from shark bites."

"How many more?" I'd asked him. But he never answered. He'd been too busy chumming the water with fish food and pointing out several shiny barracuda—the fish, not the cars— that constantly circled the boat.

Fortunately, we'd survived snorkeling at Looe Key, but I don't like to tempt fate.

"The ocean looks rough today," I cautioned my wife. "They're predicting 4-inch swells and visibility less than 50 feet."

"That's OK," I don't want to go out on the ocean today."

I smiled.

"I want to ride the Conch Train."

I unsmiled.

The Conch—aptly pronounced *konk*—Train looks like something from Toontown at Disneyland. Only instead of inching its way through throngs of little kids, this train wound its way through narrow streets full of large delivery trucks and cars being driven by overly excited people looking through camcorders.

"You're sure about that world's largest turtle shell? I hear it's breathtaking."

She handed me my ticket and we climbed aboard the train behind a guy wearing a microphone and an Evel Knievel hat.

"Welcome aboard," the guy said. "I'm Ace, and I'll be your driver today." He stomped on the gas pedal, forcing two bicyclists into a hedge. "Please, no screaming or leaping from the train."

I stopped screaming and sat back down.

"Key West has an interesting history," he began. "For instance, it was a day just like today when a fire raced right up this very street, destroying everything in its path in mere seconds."

We took a corner on 18 wheels, all on the left side of the train.

"'Course, that's nothing compared to the hurricanes of '96, '97, '98 and '99."

I thought I felt a sprinkle.

"Did I mention that we are only 90 miles from Cuba? They say we could be the first city destroyed during a nuclear attack."

The Conch Train stopped suddenly to let an old woman holding two chickens cross the street.

"That's Crazy Shirlee," Ace whispered. "She hates tourists. And they say she practices voodoo."

Shirley looked right at me and I realized I was holding 14 brochures, three bags of souvenirs and two cameras. I grabbed my wife and climbed off the train.

"Where are we going?" she asked.

"I think I've seen enough of Key West," I said.

My wife smiled. "Maybe you're right. Besides we have those discount coupons for the alligator nature walk in the Everglades."

Great. Only I hoped the alligators wouldn't realize how well-seasoned we really were.

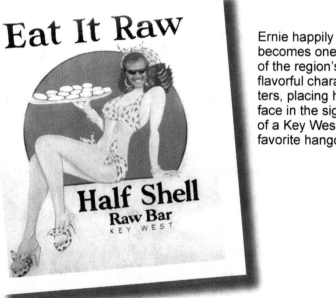

Ernie happily becomes one of the region's flavorful characters, placing his face in the sign of a Key West favorite hangout.

Check out the bar: www.halfshellrawbar.com

Geared Up in Guatemala

by
Terri Elders

My friend, Kelly, and I needed a break from La Antigua, Guatemala. Peace Corps Volunteers in neighboring Belize, we had spent our vacation strengthening our Spanish at a full immersion school in the cobble-stoned colonial city. But already we had probed every palacio, toured every *ruina*, and sampled the national dish *pepian* in dozens of *posadas*.

"Let's explore this weekend," Kelly said that Saturday noon, as he sipped a second cup of fresh-from-the-*fincas* coffee on the patio of our favorite bakery, Doña Luisa Xicotencatl. "Maybe Pana?" He glanced at me. We had discussed this before.

Panajachel sits on the shores of Lake Atitlán. Novelist Aldous Huxley once wrote, "Lake Como, it seems to me, touches on the limit of permissibly picturesque, but Atitlán is Como with additional embellishments of several immense volcanoes. It really is too much of a good thing."

Discovered by hippies in the late 1960s, Pana's natural beauty and *tipico* handicrafts attract so many tourists that locals call it *Gringotenango*. Even though "chicken bus" fares were cheap, the route still seemed risky to me, a tortuous two-hour ride through steep highland roads with blind hairpin turns. I hesitated.

"Look, we can rent a motorcycle." Kelly's voice was soothing, reassuring. "I just saw that a shop has opened near the *parque central*, by the Santa Catalina arch. Let's meander over and take a gander."

"A motorcycle?" I raised an eyebrow. "When I was 12, the only time Daddy took me on his Indian for a spin around the block I trembled for an hour afterward."

Kelly grinned. "You're not 12 now. Besides, you're a daredevil Peace Corps Volunteer! And I'm no novice. I used to ride a cycle to UCLA every morning."

I nodded. In the park a few minutes later, we passed a fountain with a deliciously indelicate mermaid. I fished in my cotton slacks for a *centavo* to toss into its murky waters. I'm Irish and I believe in luck—and asking for help from whatever mystical powers might lurk near, be they racy mermaids or Mayan deities, was OK with me.

Kelly's eyes lit up when we entered the shop. "Hey, they've got baby Yams." He walked over to a Yamaha and patted its seat. "This is a 175 DT. It's a trail bike, but with everything we need to be fully road legal." He sat astride the seat, tooted the horn and adjusted the mirrors.

"A dirt bike? Do you think it will be safe?" I frowned.

"It's got a willing, reliable engine and six gears. That's all we need."

The shopkeeper sidled up. His English exceeded our Spanish so we negotiated a reasonable two-day fee, accepted the keys and a pair of crash helmets.

I climbed behind Kelly to ride back to the *posada* where I packed my new Mayan knapsack with toiletries, underwear, tees and socks. "It's warmer at Pana so we won't need much more," Kelly said.

Still mid-afternoon, we'd reach Pana by twilight. The Maya word Atitlán means "the place where the rainbow gets its color," and I wanted to see the widely-touted sunset.

We sped along the Pan-American Highway, and the motorcycle hugged the curves. But an hour past bustling Chimaltenango, we ran into a fog bank and the air took on a biting chill. Kelly felt me shaking with cold and pulled over. We layered on our extra T-shirts and sheltered our hands with socks in lieu of mittens.

At Los Encuentros, the point where Panajachel and Chichicastenango roads converged, we stopped at a café. I wanted some hot chocolate to counter my shivers, but when the steaming cinnamon-scented mug arrived, my fingers shook so hard I could only wrap my hands around it, grateful for its warmth. Kelly, hardier, swigged a bottle of the local Gallo beer and said, "Pana's only 10 more miles. We're nearly there. We just have to keep moving."

I peered out the window into the thick morass of fog, wondering if the lake were shrouded as well. So much for the rainbowed sunset I'd hoped to witness.

We plodded on, the Yamaha chugging happily, but soon

the daylight faded away completely. I realized we were climbing. We took serpentine curve after curve on our steep ascent, at dwindling speed. Finally Kelly stopped.

"If we're heading for the lake, shouldn't we be going downhill, not up?" I asked.

"I think we missed the turnoff in the fog. But if you look up to the left, there are some lights. That might be Chichicastenango." Kelly's teeth chattered as much as mine.

"I read that Chichi's altitude is 6,500 feet. No wonder we're so cold."

"Unless we want to turn into icicles, we better keep moving forward, not turn back," Kelly said.

I clambered aboard, closed my eyes, and mentally reminded myself of that earthy Antigua mermaid that I'd bribed as our valiant dirt bike chugged, *I think I can, I think I can.*

Soon we neared stucco-white buildings on the outskirts of a darkened town and spied lights behind the shuttered doors of what resembled a monastery, but carried a sign reading "Hotel Santa Tomas." We pounded on the door. The night manager unlocked the gated entrance, offered a vacant room with twin beds, and agreed we could store our bike in the safety of the courtyard. Though the restaurant already had closed, he brought me a mug of chocolate and Kelly a couple of fingers of brandy. We sighed with contentment as we lit a fire in the enormous fireplace.

After a scalding bath, I wrapped myself in a Mayan blanket and gazed at the crackling fire while Kelly visited the bathroom. A few minutes later he joined me. "You used up all the hot water," he complained.

I sipped my chocolate and shrugged. "Sorry," I murmured. "At least we're warm here in front of the fire."

The next morning, thoroughly thawed, we hopped back on the Yamaha and departed for Pana. Our Yam hummed steadily even as it clung to the road on the spiraling 2,500-foot descent from Solola to Panajachel. But on the final turn, Kelly glanced off to the left at some women washing their laundry at the foot of a waterfall and we took a spill. Fortunately we had slowed and weren't badly hurt. I gashed my right shin, but wrapped a bandana around the wound, and we proceeded to our destination, an inn at the foot of the lake. That evening, I reveled in counting the colors of the rainbow in the sunset as I drank yet another aromatic hot chocolate.

One day 20 years later, I dug out a photo that Kelly had snapped of me standing beside the Yamaha, framed by the cones of the Atitlán volcanoes, cradling my crash helmet. I showed it to my husband.

"You rode that on the Pan-American Highway and over rough mountain roads in the dark? That's a dirt bike!" His eyes widened in disbelief.

"Well, I'm a daredevil," I explained. "Plus I had a little help from some Mayan gods, a notorious mermaid, several cups of Guate chocolate, and a cycler who insisted we keep moving forward." And we did.

Kelly snapped Terri's photo on their
weekend ride to Panajachel, located
near Lake Atitlán.

Terri has dedicated this book to Kelly.
Read page iv.

We'll Always Have Vectis

by
Joyce Newman Scott

I pulled my pink floral comforter back, threw myself on my bed, and buried my head under four down pillows. I coughed and then sneezed. "I'm not sure I'm up to this trip."

"You'll be fine," Tom said, as he sat next to me. My husband tried to lift one of the pillows from my head. "I wouldn't go without you. Wouldn't have any fun."

I wrapped my fingers tightly around the pillow. "What if my ears don't stay open on the flight over? Traveling with a sinus infection is crazy. I'm running a fever."

Tom smiled that lopsided grin he gets when he wants something. "We'll take it slow. Get plenty of rest. Sleep late. Eat great meals. Besides, we haven't had a real vacation in six months. This is the Vectis show."

My husband is an avid toy soldier collector and this was the biggest show of the year. When I first met him 28 years ago, he had never been outside sunny Florida. But I was a flight attendant and had traveled the world. By using the toys as bait, I watched as he slowly changed. And now he loved to travel—to wherever there was a toy show.

The next day as the plane descended into Charles de Gaulle Airport in Paris, I visualized the tiny Tidy Bowl man floating inside my brain on a blue raft, jabbing a red hot poker into my eardrums. Then I felt an explosion, as if a block of ice had been wrapped around my eardrums, obstructing normal sound. "I can't hear you!" I yelled.

Tom smiled and his eyes glazed over. He patted my hand. *"We're going to have such a good time. Two days in Paris. Four in London. And the toy show."* I guessed that's what he was saying as I watched his mouth move, but I'd heard nothing.

Two days later one ear popped. We were on the Eurostar speeding from Paris to London, going 120 mph through a pitch-black tunnel. The lights in the cabin dimmed. I wondered if hearing loss could also affect eyesight. Suddenly, my left eardrum felt like an atomic rocket had launched nearby. I fantasized about climbing under my fluffy down comforter at the hotel and hiding.

Later, on the cab ride over to the hotel, Tom said, "We'll just drop our bags off, then lunch at your favorite restaurant." A bribe for the upcoming toy show that he was anticipating. "Then I have a few things to pick up from the last auction. Only a minute. OK?" His face carried a childlike look of excitement over the show. There was no stopping him. I'd created a monster.

We stopped at our favorite Italian restaurant in Covent

Garden and had the usual: a bottle of Pinot Grigio and the grilled rosemary chicken. In spite of the abundant garlic, I tasted nothing. About five hours later, completely exhausted, Tom opened the door to our hotel room. He threw himself across the bed without pulling down the covers. I checked my watch: 10:30 P.M. Finally, some sleep. But first a hot shower. In the bathroom, I yanked off my clothes, bundled myself in a terry robe and turned on the faucets, breathing in the delicious steam. That's when I heard the first announcement over the loudspeaker.

"This is not an emergency. Stay calm. Repeat. It is not an emergency. Stay in your room and wait for further information." The announcement was then repeated in German, French, Italian and Japanese. On the third repeat, I shook Tom on the bed.

"Wake up!" I shouted. "We have to leave!"

Tom rolled his head to the side and opened one eye. "They said wait in your room. I'm not going anywhere." He was still dressed in jeans and lug-soled shoes.

I'm a former Eastern Airlines flight attendant. You can't tell a flight attendant who flew for 20 years to stay in her room during an emergency. I pulled on my black pants and sweater and stuffed my bra into my purse.

"Let's go." I kicked Tom's leg.

Without lifting his head, he said, "Take the toys with you. I'll stay here."

I knew better than to take the elevator during a fire, even an undeclared fire. I climbed down four flights of stairs, swearing to myself. In the lobby, people dressed in business suits sat drinking sexy blue drinks in triangular-shaped glasses as if nothing unusual had happened. Standing at the glass entrance door, I watched two red fire trucks with flashing lights pull up in front of the building. A burly fireman got off the truck, adjusted his yellow helmet and quietly asked the concierge, "Seems this has happened before?"

The concierge shrugged. "Some bloke smoking set off the fire detector."

OK, so I'm an alarmist, I thought. Still not trusting the elevators, I climbed the stairs back up to my room. Tom was asleep on the bed and snoring.

The next morning, I walked to the Vectis Toy and Figure Show and glanced around the crowded room. One long mirrored wall made the room seem gigantic. Row after row of linen-covered tables were filled with boxes of soldiers of every type: plastic, tin, modern and antique. Hundreds of people—one man in jeans, one man in a blue work shirt, another with a long tattoo running the length of his arm—all moved around the room circling the boxes, inspecting the contents, gazing at the toys like entranced children. I worked my way around the room and listened to the different accents. Before me were men and women from various countries, all enjoying the same hobby.

Tom grabbed my sweater and pulled me through a huddle of men bending over to admire lead soldiers on a table. He pointed to Andy, a jovial Englishman with an infectious laugh.

"Andy has a stand at Portobello Road!" Tom yelled over the din.

I asked Andy if I could take a picture and he beamed. He

picked up a figure of a woman on a horse. "How about with a Mignot Joan of Arc?" I was able to click my camera before Tom grabbed my hand and dragged me upstairs to the second floor, out of breath and panting. He muttered something about a good picture.

When I looked up, Tom had disappeared. I found him squirreled away at the far end of the room at a stand, a wagon locked firmly in his hand. "I'll take . . ." Tom glanced at me first. "Two motorcycles and the wagon." The proprietor of the stand fingered his graying beard.

"Where are you from?" I asked.

"Germany."

"How long have you been coming to the show?"

"Two or three years," he answered. "I usually buy more than I sell, though."

It was the same story everywhere I went. I was beginning to see the big picture. This show was about friendship, not sales. All of the collectors—American, British, Belgiun, German—were there for a reason. And it was more than money. It was friendship. They made up a sort of United Nations of the heart, with the common denominators being history and a love for the toys. That was it. The toys were actually a bridge for building international relationships. All around me, brilliant, successful men and women from all walks of life were bonding together in friendship.

Outside the toy show, a heavy rain was falling. I buttoned my jacket to protect myself from the wind. Finding a shredded hanky in my pocket, I blew my nose. I thought my sinus infection would never get better. Tom turned, gently placed a hand on my shoulder, pulled me close, and kissed me. "Thank you for coming," he whispered. "It means a lot to me."

I smiled as I pulled my jean jacket collar up around my neck. I felt a little like Ingrid Bergman in *Casablanca*.

"We'll always have Vectis," I whispered, happy that I had helped to create a world traveler.

Joyce and Tom

Smack-Dab Middle

by
Kathe Campbell

Come sunshine or blizzard, and ofttimes both, we two old duffers loved trucking over mountain and prairie, where the backcountry lured us off beaten paths onto secondary roads. Most travelers in either giant motor homes or travel trailers miss this Old West charm and the unchanged pristine landscapes—broad valleys and rolling hills dotted with cottonwoods and pines, and meandering streams that turn the grasslands green and lush for bountiful herds of deer. And here, bears, moose, elk and wily predators roam to the eerie sounds of raptors soaring and hunting against the backdrop of snow-capped peaks.

But for the blink of an eye, my husband Ken and I nearly missed a charming old country hamlet hidden behind massive lilac hedges. The sign read, "Ringling." We learned that the town's two circus brothers, who prospered in a world quite apart from whence they were conceived and reared, were its only claim to fame.

It's said that if you wait a half-hour in this region, the weather changes. We nearly froze our gizzards and wore out the windshield wipers plodding through June's slush and headwinds. While cows and calves stood hunkered against barbed wire, in anticipation of eminent relief, we pulled onto the shoulder to wait out the assault.

Surprisingly, our home-on-the-range daydreaming was interrupted by a visual ambush. Down a long curvy hill, we spied a scene smacking of young perceptions of the Old West, where the cowboys of yesteryear whooped it up after a trail drive. The remains of a tattered sign pitched by a bygone rodeo stretched across the dusty main thoroughfare, and a post office competed with an old-timer's cabin. Lastly, stepping gingerly up old dished stairs, the Cattleman's Hotel revealed dingy curtains and moldy rooms idle and unswept, along with one water-stained bath at the end of the hall.

There stood an ancient gas pump in front of a general store full of cheap trinkets and stale bread. A diner was attached to a smoke-filled saloon that reeked of stale beer. Raspy country 78 rpms plopped down on a jukebox turntable and cue sticks waited for someone to poke balls atop a pool table harboring mysterious stains. This characterized the place, for it appeared little attempt had been made to brighten and modernize the town in its heyday after men were called away for military duty.

It was noon, the blizzard had blown south, and although the scene was grim, we were curious and hungry. The diner facade sported a large Conestoga wagon wheel adorned with a tacky, flickering neon sign. Cayuses greeted us at the hitching rail as we entered the diner to laughter and the drone of men's voices—then abrupt silence. I felt compelled to belt out a chorus of *Lonesome Polecat* as the waitress rushed past, overlapping plates stacked precariously up both arms.

"Take a seat anywheres, folks," she roared. We found a table next to a window, one I doubted had ever been washed, and waited for menus until a voice in the crowd hollered, "Ain't no menus, folks, jist the chalkboard!" Sure enough, the chalkboard read: "DINNER. Soup or slaw, roast beef, taters n' gravy, slim beans, biscuts, strawberry pie, milk or coffee."

Conspicuously jammed into jeans just a wee bit tight, Opal swished between tables filling coffee cups. She was "big in the little and bottom at the top," if you know what I mean, those thighs just fightin' like a couple young'uns under a blanket with her every move. She often stooped low over a table for a few moments, and then rose up in uproarious throaty guffaws. Twice she leaned down and told a colorful story within hearing distance, and then gave us a wink as my poor Ken turned beet red.

Ken went first to a door marked "Pointers." He emerged, trying to keep a straight face. I entered the "Setters" door, the men roaring with laughter amongst themselves. Attempts at shaking up this old blue-jeaned gal failed, for I had been there, done that, in stranger places.

Meanwhile, a bunch of old-timers drew up rickety wooden chairs to our table, barely functional but for spans of twisted wire criss-crossed betwixt the legs. While leaning perilously backward, puffing on smelly rolled-up cigarettes, they entered into inquisitives with Ken. He was enjoying them thoroughly, but I was anxious to hear of their adventures spoken in characteristic drawls between dinner courses.

"Say thar, girlie. Wharin deed ya git that purty red har?" spoke an old fossil with a weathered face and no teeth. "You married to that old fella, or you his daughter?"

The meal was copious and scrumptious, creations of the grizzled and bewhiskered big Swede sweating his heart out in the sweltering kitchen. We simply could not put away the entire fare, but felt duty-bound to save room for his fresh strawberry pie piled with real whipped cream.

As long as the good Lord keeps us a travelin' pair, we'll never run out of good journaling, for the first half of life gave us the know-how, the next half supplies the impressions. What fun to befriend captivating folks and listen to the spinning of cowboy yarns, the kind that will fade away forever in this new century. It's what you call a "gen-u-ine" old cowboy happening, smack-dab in the middle of Montana.

Kathe and Ken

Tracking Hurricane Bill

by

Diana M. Amadeo

As the boot flew across the room, I conceded this would be a rough ride. Hurricane Bill was expected to hit landfall in less than 24 hours. Hubby and I had caught the last ferry available for Nova Scotia in Eastern Canada. This much-needed romantic vacation had been on our schedule for months. Come hell or high water, we'd head for the island. Funny now, about that hell and high water.

"I'm so sorry," a weary traveler said, scooping up her errant rain boot. She was decked out in splash gear and prepared for the worst. I felt almost naked in my shorts and khaki shirt.

"Is this seat saved?" she asked, hoping to ground her weaving body.

"Yes," I said, "My poor husband just took off cursing the Bonine tablet he took. No telling how long he'll be seasick."

The lady gave me a sympathetic smile and stumbled across

the forward viewing lounge, falling into the first empty seat.

The noisy room was full of travelers, most looking like natives trying to get home. Views from the boat's ceiling-to-floor windows were obscured by heavy fog and pelting rain. *So much for catching a glimpse of whales,* I thought, while settling into the lounger. I had a fleeting notion to go check up on my husband, but years of experience squashed that idea. Men have their pride. I put in my ear buds and turned on the iPod—time to listen to a good novel and veg for a while.

It ended up that my hubby had motion sickness a good four out of the five hours of the voyage. His only view, other than the gray churning ocean from the rear observation deck, was the bowl of the stainless steel potty. The lurching, jerking ride kept me seat-bound nearly the entire trip, but I made a good dent in my novel. We both avoided the dining area and the theater. The movies showing in the theater would have encouraged further upchucking, anyway. In an effort to appease a family audience and maintain a low budget, kooky B-rated movies were playing on-screen. What a crazy way to start our first vacation alone—just the two of us—in 30 years.

As my ashen, weak husband drove our car off that cursed ferry, it came to my attention that we had just spent the first five hours of our trip apart. We'd hoped this would be a bonding experience. We had a good marriage; it had survived triumphs and tragedies, birth and death, health and illness and now the inevitable sandwich generation. Two of our children had finished college, married and had children of their own. Our final child was an upper classman at MIT. Financially, it looked like we would survive the current economic downturn. Yet, in the process of living, Hubby and I had become fragmented as a couple. Our sensitivity to each other, and the world in general, had dulled.

The lighthouse route from Yarmouth wasn't the breath-taking ride that we'd hoped for. The rain had lightened, but the air was still dense and heavy from hanging fog. Anyone with heart or lung problems would have really struggled. We couldn't distinguish ocean from land. A hazy mist eerily enveloped each lighthouse and the thick and still air was downright creepy.

This was peak tourist season, but we seemed alone driving the hazy scenic highway. Every ocean-side motel posted vacancies. It was as if we were in a Stephen King movie. Evidently, most tourists had wisely canceled visiting the island because of Hurricane Bill. But Hubby and I never backed down from a challenge, even when we should have.

We reached the bed-and-breakfast in the early evening, just as the proprietors were leaving for dinner reservations elsewhere. "Oh, you came despite the storm," the owner said, sounding disappointed. "Here's a flashlight in case we lose electricity tonight. You have the third floor."

My husband had booked their only suite—a smartly reno-vated attic in the circa 1784 home. It was quaint and resembled a tiny apartment, complete with kitchen and windows that faced every direction. As luck would have it, the best view of the ocean was from the bathtub. Navigating the skinny wind-ing staircase with bulky luggage was a challenge, but the room was charming . . . and hot. There was no AC in the B&B. The heat rising to the top floor and the oppressively humid outdoor air made even the fans whine.

To our surprise, the suite had two tiny corner bedrooms, each big enough for a single bed. Other than hospitalizations, this would be our first night sleeping apart since our wedding. That night, in my tiny bed all alone, I smiled at the irony of our romantic suite. I opened the skylight over the bed in an attempt for some relief from the stifling heat. As I drifted off to sleep, I wondered if this old place were haunted . . . and if the departed were angry or happy. Casper the Friendly Ghost was playing in my dreams when I felt a familiar spooning behind me. I snuggled back to the warm body and turned to welcome Hubby—but no one was there.

I was awakened again about 2 A.M. by howling wind and water pouring on my face, thanks to the opened skylight. Bill had arrived in all his fury. The overhead skylight immediately closed by itself due to the 65 mph winds. Over that wind and the downpour, I could hear my husband snoring in the next room. Putting my standby earplugs in place, I fell back asleep in my damp bed.

"Did you hear the storm come in?" my husband asked the next morning while watching the downpour.

How could I have missed it? I thought. He didn't listen for my response as he mapped our day's drive. "The storm might slow us down a bit."

"There's no rush," I said softly, knowing full well that we were following the direct route of Bill.

That morning at breakfast, the proprietor shook her head at our desire to head to Halifax. I smiled at the irony. She was a native—why would she know more than us? We packed up our gear and headed to the car in the blinding rain. Hurricane, hell—we had survived tornadoes in Iowa.

The air smelled like fish. There were no cars on the washed-out roads. Debris created hazard conditions. Road crews frowned as they stepped back to allow us through. The wind was fierce, but our car was winning the fight. Good Old Reliable. We continued on the Lighthouse route as the eye of the hurricane allowed the winds to subside and the sun to peek through. What we saw of the distant coastline heightened our perception of nature's majestic force. The incredible crashing waves begged for a closer look.

We found a dirt road off the highway marked "Shoreline Road." Dodging fallen limbs and deep water-filled ruts, we drove until we could no longer continue. The ocean had swallowed the beach and the very road we were on.

"Oh my God," Hubby exclaimed. I merely gasped.

An old shed to our left was partially submerged in high tide. To our right were boulders that had been thrown from the sea. What was left of the beach and road before us was a mass of debris and tangled seaweed. In the calm of the eye, we sprang from the car for a closer look.

The storm surge had arrived with the high tide, creating rough seas and 30-foot-high thunderous waves. We stepped back in awe. These elements demanded respect. In the distance, we could briefly view Peggy's Cove and the lighthouse that literally and repeatedly was being consumed by waves.

We laughed as ocean water sprayed over us and giggled like teenagers of long ago. We were foreigners watching a once-in-a-lifetime event unfold in front of our very eyes. I took my husband's hand and leaned into his body. Then we heard an odd high-pitched sound.

"What was that?" I asked.

"It came from over there," Hubby said, motioning toward a mound of seaweed. The mound moved. "There's something alive in there."

Curiosity overpowered hesitation. We abandoned the fantastic sight before us and began to tug at the seaweed. What would we uncover? A rodent, a live Montauk monster, an errant seagull? A large and absurdly-shaped bill with brightly colored red, blue and yellow markings poked out, fronting little weary eyes that blinked in the sun.

"A parrot?' I asked, stupidly.

"Oh, wow, it's a puffin," my husband answered, as the seabird struggled forth from its bondage. "It must have gotten thrown off track by the hurricane."

We watched as the dazed puffin fully emerged, shook itself off and waddled down the muddy road before taking flight. It raised high over the waves before diving into the churning waters below.

Behind me, a familiar body snuggled close. A pair of arms wrapped around my waist and a soft kiss landed behind my ear. *Ah, at last!*

I turned around into my husband's embrace. Nova Scotia during a hurricane . . . what could be more romantic?

The Williamsburg Shuffle

by
Annmarie B. Tait

My husband, Joe, and I have enjoyed Williamsburg, Virginia, as our getaway spot for many years—30 to be exact. We went there for the first time in 1982 on a friend's recommendation.

Back then, we were both single and looking for something affordable within driving distance of Philadelphia. A Williamsburg brochure arrived one morning in the mail, depicting a living history Mecca that offered package plans, including lodging and meals. The town featured beautiful scenery, a variety of museums, live entertainment nightly, and, as a bonus, Busch Gardens. We were sold on a Williamsburg vacation before we got to the third page of the glossy guide.

About two years after we started dating, my husband joined the Navy. It was not an easy decision for him to make or for me to accept, but Joe was determined that the Navy offered training and opportunities for education he otherwise could not afford. So I stood waving goodbye on the East Coast as he left for boot camp on the West Coast. Would this relationship stand the test of time and distance? Who knew? We were not engaged. I'd just moved into my first apartment, and though he stayed with me most of the time, his address of record still was his mother's home. *What would ever become of us?* I wondered.

Through boot camp and all of his other training, Joe and I wrote each other faithfully. It was the early 1980s, and email and cell phones did not yet exist. Long distance phone calls were expensive. Pen and paper came pretty cheap at Woolworth's, and writing all those letters took considerable time and attention. As the months passed, the letters took a more serious tone. Marriage seemed inevitable, though neither of us ever mentioned getting engaged.

About a year after he enlisted, Joe was able to schedule leave, so he asked me to book a vacation for us in Williamsburg. It had been 12 long months of not seeing one another, and saving expensive long distance calls only for special occasions.

"I'll be home in three days, Annie. Make sure you book dinner at the fanciest restaurant they have. We're going in style, so bring a pretty dress to wear and I'll put on my dress uniform."

"I'll put on my dress uniform" should have been a big fat tipoff that Joe had special plans. Ordinarily when not on duty, he wouldn't get caught dead in his uniform. At the time, though, that little nugget of foreshadowing eluded me. All I heard was "pretty dress" and "fancy dinner."

"You can count on me, Joe. I'll make all the arrangements."

I hung up the phone and immediately dialed 1-800-HIS-TORY and made a reservation for us at the Williamsburg

Lodge Hotel for five nights. This included dinner each evening at a different colonial tavern, with a final reservation at the grand Williamsburg Hotel Regency Room. The Regency Room was a bona fide five-star restaurant featuring captain's service, a dance floor with a three-piece jazz ensemble, impeccable French cuisine and a wine sommelier. I ask you, could a 20-something chick who had a date at a five-star restaurant with a guy in uniform ask for more? I don't think so!

Over the course of the next few days, I packed. And I packed and I packed and I packed some more. I packed jeans, shorts, dress slacks, a couple of casual skirts, tops, blouses, T-shirts, a shawl for the evenings, a couple of light-weight sweaters, a different dress for each dinner, two bathing suits, sneakers, sandals, flip-flops and five different pairs of dress shoes for my dinner ensembles, each with a matching handbag. But then I reconsidered. With it being August, when you can cut the humidity with a knife in Virginia, I removed the sweaters. I had to. I needed room for the jewelry.

Three suitcases, one duffle bag and two and a half days later, I still hadn't packed one single item for Joe, and he was due home in only a few hours. So I threw open a fourth suitcase and tossed in undies, sweat socks, T-shirts, one pair of casual pants, a few pairs of shorts, swim trunks, a dress shirt or two, and his shaving kit. Case closed, literally. All that was left was to wait patiently for Joe to arrive. As I sat there, it occurred to me that for Joe to volunteer to wear his dress uniform, some big plans must be been at stake. *Could it be? Was he going to ask me to . . . ?* Nah, we were serious, but not that kind of serious yet. Or were we?

After Joe's grand arrival home, we got up bright and early the next morning and set out for Williamsburg. We talked nonstop, but nary a word about our future. *OK,* I thought, *you're making a big deal out of nothing. The man just wants to make a nice memory for you. This dinner is the highpoint of our trip, not getting engaged. Get used to it.*

Williamsburg proved to be all we'd hoped for. We enjoyed exploring the historical sites, splashing around at the hotel pool, touring museums, shopping, hiking, taking a cruise on the Chesapeake Bay and visiting Busch Gardens. After the sun went down, we'd whisk off to one of various colonial taverns where we'd dine on sumptuous authentic 18th-century fare served by waiters in period costumes. Each tavern featured a variety of diversions, running the gamut from colonial jesters, magicians and folk singers to trained classical musicians playing replica instruments. So romantic, and we were building up to this wonderful five-star restaurant evening. But I still secretly hoped for a surprise with sparkle.

As I dressed for dinner on the big day, I wondered how I'd get rid of the butterflies in my stomach before we sat down to eat. I needed room for all that five-star food. Hard as I tried to calm down, the jitters had a strong hold on me. To distract myself, I decided to stroll to the lobby gift shop, so I told Joe that's where he could find me when he was ready.

About 15 minutes later, I stood perusing a rack of postcards when I looked up as the lobby elevator doors opened. I'd never seen Joe in his dress whites. Even to this day, that sight is clear in my mind's eye. He took my breath away, until he stepped off the elevator and hesitantly stepped forward. Each step looked like an adventure in pain. Or as if he sported a self-inflicted atomic wedgie. I rushed to his side.

"Joe, what's wrong? Did you wrench your back?"

"Nothing, Annie. Nothing's wrong. Let's get going."

"You sure you're OK? You're walking awfully, um, weird."

"Stop asking questions, Annie," he said, teeth slightly clenched. "I told you I'm fine. Now let's go, or we'll be late."

The restaurant was just across the street from our hotel—a mere 90-second walk for the average pedestrian. I, however, happened to be on the arm of Rear Admiral Slow-Mo. If I'd known it was going to take that long to cross the street, I'd have packed a snack.

"Joe, people are starting to point and snicker. WHAT is the problem? Are you sick?"

"Not in the least," he replied, as an elderly man and his wife with her walker passed us.

"OK, if you say you're good, I believe you. No more questions. I promise."

I'd decided that perhaps he'd thought of proposing, but at the last minute terror had swept him into a full nelson lock, cutting off circulation to his legs. This engagement thing was not meant to be—that's all there was to it.

I shoved those thoughts aside as we crept up to the maître d'. Joe stood straight and tall, his hat now tucked under his left arm, as he crooked his right arm to escort me.

"Joe Beck, party of two," he said, confidently.

"Very good, Mr. Beck, I have your reservation. Follow me, please."

The maître d' sailed across the empty dance floor like a

swan on a lake while we, the crippled-by-God only knows-what couple, hobbled along behind him. All hands on deck cast a sorrowful glance at the Navy veteran, obviously nursing a combat injury. Only I knew that he hadn't even set foot on a ship yet. The guys in the Colonial Fife and Drum Corps were more at risk for a battle injury than Joe. He'd spent the last year in one training facility after another.

When we finally arrived at our table, the maître d' pulled out my chair with one hand and with the other, snapped the napkin from its fanciful folds and placed it ever so gently on my lap. Meanwhile, Joe shimmied around to the other side of the table and slithered into the chair, tucking his legs under the table with all speed. The pained expression on his face melted into one of pure relief.

"Everything OK, Joe?"

"Yep. I'm good."

Joe ordered champagne, and as the dinner progressed, he gradually relaxed, but he never budged one inch from his chair, not even to visit the restroom. I was dying to twirl around the dance floor in my blue-and-green silk dress with puffy sleeves and full skirt, but Joe's butt was superglued to the seat.

After a delicious meal, accompanied by a superb jazz trio, it was time to leave. Thinking about having to inch our way back to our hotel due to Joe's unexplainable malady did not thrill me. We headed toward the door, with Joe still shuffling and me on his arm, smiling sweetly at those who'd missed our entry.

Once through the lobby doors and under the cover of darkness, Joe regained full use of his legs. I didn't hear any background harps, but a miracle had taken place before my very eyes.

"Joe, you've recovered!"

"Recovered from what? There's nothing wrong with me. Why don't we go for a walk, Annie? It's a beautiful evening."

Apparently I'd turned a perfectly normal boyfriend over to the United States Navy, and they'd sent me back a dashing young split personality, dressed in a crisp white uniform with spit-shined shoes.

"Sure, Joe, I'd love to take a walk."

We headed up the street toward the Governor's Palace. A lovely breeze gave relief from the humidity, and the full moon was beautiful. After a bit, we sat down on a bench to enjoy the stunning stars overhead. Joe turned to me.

"Annie, the next time we go on vacation, I'm sending you a checklist so you don't forget anything."

"I forgot something? I packed everything but the kitchen sink."

With that, I looked down as Joe inched up his pants legs, revealing that he'd worn a pair of my suntan knee-high hosiery.

"Socks, Annie, you might want to pack some dress socks for me as long as you want to be in charge of the packing."

We both doubled over with laughter. He'd been so afraid to move, fearing that someone would notice he was wearing women's knee-high nylons. Aside from being out of uniform, you'd have to admit that if he'd been hit by a bus, it would have been a pretty hard thing to explain in the hospital emergency room.

When the laughter died down, I looked at him again. He handed me a small red, heart-shaped velvet box.

"This is for you, Annie."

I opened it to find the most exquisite antique diamond,

sparkling in a high filigree platinum setting. It was magnificent and so was the guy who would go through such antics just so he could make good on his promise to wear his dress uniform for our special date.

I don't think he ever officially asked me to marry him, nor did I ever say I would. I put on the ring and have never taken it off, except for the day we were married 29 years ago, when I removed it only long enough for Joe to slip on my wedding band.

We will return to Williamsburg in just a few weeks to enjoy its scenery, hospitality and whatever new exhibits it has to offer. I'm sure we'll dine at a few lovely restaurants. Most people will look at us and see an average couple in their mid-50s. But me? I'll be on the arm of a dashing young man in his dress whites.

There'll be no shuffling, though. When I pack for vacations these days, I start with the dress socks.

Annmarie

Spanglish

by
Jennifer Martin

A few years ago, my husband, Bud, and I were planning to go on a Mediterranean cruise. I had studied Spanish in college, but Bud had never taken a foreign language class, not even in high school. Since our first stop was Barcelona, and we'd be spending a few pre-cruise days there, I thought he should learn a bit of Spanish, so I bought him an expensive set of beginning Spanish tapes. He had retired a few years earlier and had lots of time to play the tapes at home and in his car. I was happy to see he'd finally be learning the rudiments of a foreign language. Or so I thought.

I was still working at the time, so often when I'd come home after a long, tiring day from school where I was a high school administrator, he'd greet me with a friendly *camisa*!(shirt), *autobus*!(bus) or some other word he'd learned that day. He was really good at rolling his R's, too, uttering *national del ferrocarrilo* every chance he got, although why he thought he'd need to say "national railroad" during our cruise vacation was beyond me. However, I felt assured he was making progress. By the time we'd get to Spain, I was sure he'd be able to master a simple conversation in Spanish.

Soon we were on the plane headed for Europe. I couldn't wait to hear him show off what he had learned. We went out to dinner the first night we were there, and I thought Bud would be able to order our meal in Spanish. But the waiter spoke to us in perfect English, blowing Bud's chance to take advantage of his newly acquired linguistic skills.

On our second day in a hotel room in Barcelona, though, Bud accidentally dropped a glass on the marble bathroom floor, scattering shards everywhere. He tiptoed out into the bedroom to tell me.

"Now's your chance to use your Spanish," I told him. "See if you can find someone to help clean up the mess."

"Right," he said, smiling tightly. "I'll be right back."

He went out into the hallway and motioned for a hotel maid to come into the room. Then he pointed to the bathroom and stammered, "Uh . . . uh . . ." Finally, he summoned up all of his newfound Spanish speaking ability, pantomimed dropping a glass, and blurted out, "POW!"

"Si, si," the maid said as she scurried away to bring back her cleaning cart.

"Pow?" I asked, incredulously. "I spent all that money on tapes and that's all you could say? Pow isn't even Spanish."

"Well, I never got around to learning any verbs. Just the

nouns," he admitted. "But it worked, didn't it? That maid and I communicated quite well. She understood me perfectly."

I wanted to slap the smirk right off his *cara* (face).

After Spain, we went on to tour France, Italy and Greece. In France, Bud got kicked out of a bar when he asked for a bottle of water in Spanish because he didn't know French, and he thought they wouldn't appreciate English. We ended up getting bottled water at a McDonald's in Nice. But he had no trouble ordering limoncello in Italy because it was pronounced just like the Spanish would say it. And he guzzled it just like he thought they would. Such an honorable gesture, wouldn't you say?

It's been years since that Mediterranean cruise, but Bud still likes to practice Spanish, especially in restaurants, using words like *ensalada* (salad) and *pollo* (chicken)—all so he can claim to everyone that he's bilingual.

I just smile, secretly glad that he hasn't quite figured out that his Spanglish is the real reason we only visit English-speaking countries now. Lately, though, I've noticed he's been saying *aloha* and *mahalo* a lot, so perhaps he's gearing up linguistically for another trip to Hawaii.

Heads turn when I call him "Paki," his Hawaiian name. Paki means Bud, but the kind of bud the Hawaiians think of when they hear that is *paki lolo* or "crazy bud," another name for marijuana. Now that I think about it, Paki Lolo fits him perfectly.

Paki Lolo (Bud) and Jennifer

CHAPTER THREE

Anchors Away!

Ahoy, mate! Ready for adventure?

High Stakes
on the High Seas

by
Pamela Frost

Cruising is my idea of the perfect vacation. The long drea-ry winters of Northeastern Ohio make the Caribbean feel like another planet. From the minute I step onto that big steel tube called an airplane with other escapees and we go hurtling into the air, defying gravity, the magic begins. My face hurts from smiling so much. We take off in snow and land among swaying palm trees, bright sunshine and heat rising from the tarmac. The taxi ride from the airport to the dock seems to take for-ever, and I resist the urge to take up my children's car chant, "Are we there yet?"

Everyone who knows anything about cruise ships knows about the amazing food and exotic ports of call. White sug-ary sand beaches are kissed by vivid turquoise surf as warm as bathwater. Snorkeling and shopping are my favorite shore ex-cursions. Both are world class in the Caribbean.

I'm frequently asked, "Don't you get bored when you're at sea all day?"

I laugh. Every night a schedule for the next day is slid under the door of our cabin and the hard part is picking what to do. Bingo, shuffleboard, karaoke, dance lessons, cooking classes, poolside games and tours of the inner workings of the ship, just to name a few activities.

Sometimes, though, all I want to do is curl up with a book at poolside while good-looking young men bring me drinks. Lately I've discovered a new passion on the cruise ship—the casino. I'm a very lucky woman.

On our last day at sea, I registered for the blackjack tournament. I wandered into the casino feeling a little shell shocked. I was exhausted from sightseeing and snorkeling the day before in Jamaica. The climb up Dunn's River Falls left my legs feeling wobbly. Bells, flashing lights and bright colors put me on sensory overload. Thinking about the tournament made me nervous, so I used my supreme willpower to stop my hands from trembling. Rubbing my sweaty palms repeatedly on the thighs of my khaki shorts, I tried to walk off some excess energy and get comfortable in this slot machine jungle.

Late afternoon was usually a dead time in a casino, but the cool and inviting air conditioning sucked my rivals in. Trying to be unobtrusive—as unobtrusive as a long-legged redhead can be—I watched the men and women approach the cashier's cage to sign up for the tournament.

I've played blackjack all my life—my daddy taught it to me as a counting game. Online games now feed my addiction. This was only my second tournament. On our last cruise I was dealt good cards, but was eliminated quickly because I was betting conservatively. This time I wouldn't make that mistake. I played the computer version of the game in the casino every night. I never got ahead and that kept me humble, but I could see patterns of probability. Card counting is such a dirty phrase.

When they announced that the tournament was about to begin, I left the computer to watch. I stood frozen as the eager beavers rushed to the table and parked their tails on the red leather bar stools. The dealer set $1,000 in chips in front of each player and fixed the maximum bet at $500. The players at this table were all conservative and the dealer was wiping them out left and right. At the end of seven hands, this group was only in the $1,000 range.

This sent my confidence soaring. I sat down in the second group. Remembering the guy who won on the last cruise— by betting the limit every time and doubling down as often as he could—my mantra became "Bet the limit—don't bust."

I took a deep breath to calm myself, but the thick cigarette smoke had the opposite effect. I looked down at my lucky rings sparkling in the bright casino lights and picked up my chips. I fingered my little stack and asked the dealer, "What's the maximum bet?"

He looked a little shocked. I could tell he didn't figure me for a high roller. I was too nervous. He hesitated ever so slightly and answered, "$500." I slapped a red $500 chip on the table. A little gasp went up from the spectators behind me.

On my table, the dealer busted over and over. A lucky break for us players. Everyone did well. At the end of seven hands, I had $4,500 and was $1,000 ahead of anybody else.

Through the next 10 tables of seven people, I remained perched like a vulture, kneeling on a bar stool for a better view of the cards. Delighted that no one was getting close to my total, my mind focused on the players' strategies and how the cards were falling, looking for the patterns.

For the final round, the top seven money winners were brought back to the table. I was still on top, so I chose my seat first. Without hesitation, I sat in the number five chair, even though everyone around me was babbling about how the last chair was the best. I'd sat in chair number five the first time and had no intentions of messing with my karma. The cards had fallen very well for me. If they continued to fall that well, I knew I could win. The top three winners would get a cash prize. I wanted to be number one.

We all started out with $1,000 in chips again. The dealer wiped out the table pretty fast. There were just three of us for the last two hands and we were all very close in money totals.

Mr. Miami Beach sat next to me, a tan, well-fed gentleman with white hair and lots of gold chains. He was gnawing on an expensive-smelling cigar and had the confidence of a pro.

Next to him was an Australian gentleman with a silky voice I could have listened to all day. He had sandy brown hair and looked ruggedly ageless and self-assured. Everyone else in the casino gathered around to watch the action. I felt the heat of their bodies pressing in behind me.

All three of us were still in for the final hand.

The dealer had an eight showing. With the way the cards were falling, I had a strong feeling that he had a face card under there.

The Aussie hunk had a nine and a face card showing for

19, and stayed on his $500 bet.

Mr. Miami took quite a bit of time to calculate his move. He had two face cards, for 20, probably a winner. He could split them and take a hit on each face card and hope for two winners, betting the limit on each to maximize his money. After carefully counting the chips in front of me and the pile in front of the bloke on his right, he decided to stay, play it safe.

I had an ace and a six, for seven or 17. Not a great hand, but still most people would probably stay. After all, the dealer had an eight showing. Odds were good I already had him beat, but not good enough for me. The dealer had been incredibly lucky up to this point, but he might have to take a hit and bust. Regardless of the outcome, I was in the money. It was just a matter of how much.

While the gentleman next to me was doing his calculations, I had been doing a few of my own. I knew if Mr. Miami didn't split, I could double down and win enough money to be in first place.

I pried my tongue off the roof of my mouth and went for the glory. The dealer turned and locked his eyes with mine, challenging me. I licked my lips, picked up a $500 chip and laid it on the table in front of me. I said, without flinching, "Double down."

A collective gasp went up across the room. A crooked smile slid across my face because I knew. I couldn't believe they couldn't see it. If I got a high card I added seven, if I got a low card I added 17. I would take third place if the bet failed, and first place if I succeeded. Go big or go home.

Now it was showdown time. My mouth tasted like I'd

been sucking on pennies. The dealer slid one card out of the shoe; this was it, my one card, face down for double the money. A thousand dollars rode on this one card. Since I was the last player, he paused only slightly for dramatic effect and then flipped it over.

Every eye in the place was glued to that card—except mine. I couldn't look. I stared into the dealer's intense blue eyes for my answer. Shock registered in his eyes.

"I don't believe it," echoed from behind me.

I finally looked down and saw the four of hearts. I felt as if my heart would leap out of my chest and join it there on the green felt.

"Twenty-one!" the dealer shouted. He flipped his face card over for 18. First place was all mine. I had won.

"How did you know?" the dealer gasped. I wanted to tell him that the Card Gods had told me so, but my head was spinning with excitement and my body was buzzing with adrenaline. I quickly rubbed the palms of my hands on my lap when I suddenly remembered the purchase I had made earlier during our trip in Jamaica. With nearly everyone in the casino waiting for my answer, I blurted out, "I had to win! I'm wearing my lucky thong!"

Priceless

by
Dahlynn McKowen

Shock. I distinctly remember the looks on their faces when those retired peace officers realized it had been one of their own who nearly won the Carmen Miranda look-alike contest.

In 2004, my husband, Ken, and I had joined 33 friends for a cruise of the western Caribbean. Ken had just retired after a 30-year career with California State Parks, starting as a ranger, and then working at headquarters in Sacramento in a number of positions, including marketing and PR, and finishing as the state's trails program manager. Most of our group consisted of State Park retirees—both men and woman—with the majority having spent their careers in the law enforcement side of the department.

Earlier that warm, sunny and perfect day, the boat docked at our first port-of-call—Cozumel, an island off Mexico's Yucatan Peninsula. Our group split up, some to shop, some to sightsee, and some simply to lounge in the local watering holes. Many of us reunited in the afternoon at a dockside restaurant to share our day's adventures. After drinking several margaritas and partaking in the local cuisine, we all made our way back to the ship.

Since we'd eaten in Cozumel, Ken and I decided to pass on the ship's usual big dinner. Most of our friends concurred, and so we agreed to meet up top at the poolside bar later that evening for drinks and appetizers. We retired to our stateroom, napped to sleep off the tequila, and then cleaned up for an evening of deck-side fun.

When Ken and I arrived on the pool deck, it was evening. The stars shone in all their brilliance, the boat churned toward our next stop, reggae music blasted from the speakers—and the entire ship's population seemed ready for a party. We spotted a few from our group here and there, but many were missing, presumably still in their staterooms.

As we crossed the deck, we heard a guy on the nearby stage say over a microphone, "Ladies, who wants to volunteer their husbands?" I instantly shouted, "Me!" Of course I didn't know why he wanted husbands. Ken shot me an oh-shit look as the host, decked out in fake dreadlocks and faking a Jamaican accent, excitedly pulled him up on stage. Three more husbands reluctantly joined him, all embarrassed when they learned their roles in this game.

We were to return to our staterooms, dress our husbands as Carmen Miranda, and then get them back to the stage, all under 15 minutes. Carmen had been a popular '40s movie star known as the Brazilian Bombshell, famous for singing and samba dancing in her signature fruit-hat outfits.

Suddenly, our travel companion and dear friend Jackie was at my side. "Let's do this," she said, thrilled to help out. And another lady joined us—a Scotswoman named Anne. When the host started the clock, the four of us took off for our stateroom, three decks down.

Once in our room, we stripped Ken to his boxer underwear. Poor Anne—who we didn't know—was embarrassed by all of this, but Jackie and I just howled. Jackie and Ken were longtime friends, having both graduated from the ranger academy together in the 1970s. Trying to contain our laughter, we slipped one of my red satin bras onto him, but it was too small to clasp, so we used a safety pin in the back. Anne suggested we put lipstick on him and ran to her room to get some, and Jackie went to her room to get a hat and some fruit—we were dressing Carmen Miranda, remember?

When Anne returned with her makeup, she asked how we knew Jackie, and we told her we were there with a group from California State Parks. Anne stopped cold. "We're here with the Chavez's, as their guests." She was talking about Carl Chavez and his wife, Margaret, who were part of our group. Anne and her traveling companion hadn't met the rest of the group yet, and had planned on doing so that very evening. When Jackie returned with her hat and one lone banana, we shared the news with her. At that point, Anne was no longer embarrassed by Ken's near nakedness and happily applied makeup to his face, including hot red lipstick, rouge, eye shadow and mascara.

In less than 15 minutes, we had turned my handsome husband into a floozy, complete with the red bra, a Japanese silk robe that he left open to expose the bra and most of his stomach, a bright green sarong wrapped around his hips, sparkling jewelry and a straw hat with one banana stuck in it. Ken drew the line at high heels and opted to go barefoot. But he did grab two apples before we left our room, putting one in each cup of the bra, giving him round, firm breasts.

With hardly any time to spare, we all dashed back upstairs where an assistant grabbed the four contestants and secluded them in a holding room until they were brought to the stage, one by one. Anne, Jackie and I made our way back to the deck to await the pageant. Then I spied the missing fellow retirees standing on the deck above, leaning over the rails to get a better view of the show.

Ken was the second of the look-alikes to be paraded to the stage. My clown-of-a-husband sashayed out, swinging his hips and acting coy with any man within reach. The audience went crazy. As the host interviewed him, Ken flirted like crazy with the young man, who, embarrassed, could barely keep his face straight. For his grand finale Ken plucked an apple from his bra and offered the host a bite of his temporary boob. When the host passed, Ken shrugged toward the audience, took a bite himself and stuffed the apple back in his bra. The crowd roared, including the guys up top. Unfortunately, Ken didn't win the contest, losing to a candidate who had donned high heels. He should have listened to us girls.

After the contest, the group reconnected. Those retired peace officers had no idea that it was their Ken who had been on stage, their Ken who brought the house down with his impersonation, their Ken who had fooled even them. To this day, I wish I had a camera to capture that one priceless moment, as a picture indeed is worth a thousand words.

Top: Dahlynn and Ken following the contest.

Bottom: Ken flirting with the girls at the ship's front desk.

Ordering À la Carte

by
Linda O'Connell

I'd heard what people do on cruise ships and I wanted no part of the decadence. I'd gone online and viewed photos of scrumptious food served in elegant dining rooms and buffet lines, and I learned that two of my favorite foods—pizza and ice cream—were available 24 hours a day. "Ten pounds average weight gain," my friends warned. I didn't need 10 pounds to round me out. As it was, I couldn't tell my butt from my gut.

Taking a cruise to the Eastern Caribbean wasn't on my priority list—heights frightened me and open seas made me quiver. I feared public dining, especially after the Norovirus had invaded the ship my friend had been on. I couldn't imagine being sick on top of being seasick. My husband reasoned that because the virus had struck, the cruise ships would be more diligent in annihilating the germs onboard, thus this would be the safest time to cruise. So off we headed.

We drove south to the Alabama coast and boarded a ship that was longer than the big box store we shopped at. I was certain that once I looked down eight stories over the balcony, I would be providing fish food for the lunkers lurking portside. As it happened, I looked down in amazement at the throng of people boarding the ship. I wasn't nauseated, but maybe a little queasy from the idea of being out to sea without so much as a Gilligan's-type island in sight. But once the captain blasted the ship's horn, it was too late. We were off and sailing.

My husband and I huffed and puffed up four flights of stairs and meandered around the ship, learning the layout. Just when we thought we had located our assigned dining room, we discovered it was another flight up. We marched back up another flight of stairs into the balcony area and located our table, which was set for 10. I was nervous about dining with eight other people, but we five couples—middle age to senior—became fast friends and created our own sitcom hilarity.

My husband and I, the Midwesterners, were actually considered Northerners by the Southerners. The men twanged about their hunting rifles, and they asked my husband if he, too, was preparing for deer season. When he said he wasn't much of a hunter, one of the guys said, "Well, let me speak for the rest of us. You all might regard deer as Bambi up there where you're from. We hunt and eat Bambi. OK? Bambi is our food."

Smile and nod. We aren't confrontational people. I kept my eyes on the menu and wondered what this guy would think of ordering roast duck, leg of lamb or shrimp cocktail. He turned out to be a meat-and-potatoes guy. At every meal, he ordered a chunk of red and a pile of potatoes—baked, sliced or mashed.

One evening, the straight-laced fellow who was used to eating deep-fried catfish saw that broiled fish was on the menu. He asked the waiter, who spoke little English, if he could have his fish fried. The waiter said, "Fish in the broiler." Our tablemate, getting more frustrated by the minute, raised his voice and surely his blood pressure. "Buddy, what I want is fish, fried-fried-FRIED!! You understand I want fried-fried-fried?"

The waiter smiled and nodded. When our food arrived, delectable-looking meals were placed in front of each of us. Just when our friend's blood pressure had returned to the normal range, he saw the waiter headed in his direction with a plate piled eight inches high with a mountain of french fries. We women caught it first. There was no entrée—this was his meal. We tried to avoid looking at him, but when we looked at each other, one of us snickered, and then the other started, then our husbands guffawed. We laughed so hard we couldn't eat. Our serious tablemate didn't crack a smile and his wife sat rigid. We knew we were being rude, but the expression on this guy's face made us howl. We were quite a spectacle, snorting and wiping away tears of laughter.

The waiter rushed over and asked if he had made a mistake.

"Forget it! I'll take a cup of coffee."

The waiter apologized and returned with a cup of coffee. Our buddy swilled a slug and spat, wiped his mouth and called the waiter over. "Come here and give me your finger!"

The waiter smiled and asked, "You want fish now?"

"No! I want your finger. Stick it in this coffee."

The waiter drew his fingers up into his uniform sleeve. Then our tablemate stabbed his own index finger to the bottom of the cup of coffee. "It's cold-cold-cold."

"You want hot-hot-hot fish? NO? More fries, sir?"

None of us could finish our meals. There was never a lack of food on board, but there was a definite lack of communication that evening.

My husband and I have been on four cruises since then, but our first cruise has been the most memorable, because along with our yummy food selections, we were served a dish of hilarity, à la carte.

No Bad Juju Allowed

by

Sheree Nielsen

It was late August 1995 and our 65-foot sailboat—the *Morning Star* of Blackbeard's Cruises—was departing the balmy island of Bimini after a much-needed night of socializing at the Compleat Angler in Alice Town. It had been a rough trip, only two good days of diving out of six, because of the weather. Studying the flooded main street, a group of us decided to wade calf-deep to check local stores for rain gear in preparation for our journey home, which would be cut short by the rising storm front. Once secured with our protective garb, we garnered one final look at Bimini, sighed and waved our last goodbye.

Despite all the unpredictable weather, I don't believe either Gilligan or Skipper experienced as much fun as we did. We were a motley crew, 23 scuba divers and six crewmembers in all. Eleven of us hailed from St. Louis, with the remainder coming from Los Angeles, Philly, Chicago and Arkansas.

The *Morning Star* set sail early Thursday afternoon for Miami. The crew hoped an early jump on things would enable us to bypass the tropical storm that was headed in our direction. They were dead wrong. Gale winds and 25-foot wind swells pummeled the sailboat, as we huddled body-to-body on deck in our rain jackets and shorts. The wind was biting cold and our jackets were rendered useless from the forces of the unforgiving sea. Our legs suffered the worst exposure, becoming red and goose-bumped. We had two choices, neither of which was particularly fantastic—stay on deck and wait out the storm, or retreat to the comfort of the galley below and suffer the consequences of seasickness.

Yessiree, we were smack dab in the middle of Tropical Storm Jerry.

After four hours on deck in the torrential rain and constant boat rocking, I heard the first mate, say to the captain, "We just went an hour and a half in the wrong direction!"

If that wasn't bad enough, the fuel pump went out. After we digested this information, frustration set in. I was weary and chilled to the bone. My throat was aching from the group sing-along of show tunes and TV jingles in an effort to stay positive and to divert attention away from the gale winds and bitterly cold, salty sea air. Shortly after we began singing the *Gilligan's Island* theme song, though, the crew became extremely agitated. They said it was bad *juju* to sing that song. When we asked what that phrase meant, they assured us that if we had to ask we didn't need to be singing that song.

Just shy of sunset, I was the first to retreat to the galley in an attempt to warm my bones. It was pointless to return to my bunk as I'd been informed the port side of the bow had major leaks. Once inside the galley, our cook greeted me. She opened my right hand and dropped wrapped treats in my palm.

"Suck peppermints . . . it will keep you from getting sick."

I quickly devoured six or seven. My tummy filled with the cool mint menthol that satisfied my soul.

Then the ship hit an incredibly large wind swell, which caused the stove to break loose from the wall in the galley. Out the window went our chance for a Bahamian dinner of lobster caught during a previous day of diving. Sipping my Constant Comment tea from a quaint ceramic mug, and munching saltines and scones while seated on the wooden bench at the galley table, my eyes widened as I watched the 30-cup coffee maker take flight across the room, wreaking havoc to anything in its path. I thanked the Lord that it had been empty.

Next, a tray of heavy silverware that included sharp steak knives plummeted airborne above my head, as gracefully as the Flying Wallendas. *Hmmm, this is interesting,* I thought, casually sipping my tea and nibbling my scones, unfazed by the silverware circus.

One by one, my fellow shipmates retreated to the galley, unable to endure the whipping icy air. Soon all of us had gathered at the community table. We chatted, visited, shared stories and maintained positive spirits, while our crew dealt with the concerns at hand. We dined on saltines, cookies, instant mashed potatoes, cream cheese and microwaved SpaghettiOs.

If we craved peanut butter, we need not ask for it if the ship was rocking. The 5-pound plastic tub was "back at ya" as it slid from one end of the table to the other as if it were possessed. We laughed and cajoled, except for the mates who were reduced to drinking Sanka. Cranky, they desired fresh coffee. We laughed even more.

My fellow shipmates and I began to feel lightheaded and nauseated once the fumes of the fuel pump filtered into the galley. The crew hurried to fix this problem. Probably not our brightest decision, but certainly the easiest—we all chose to take a nap. Many of us with wet sleeping quarters were offered a bunk-share with others who were willing to give up a portion of their personal space.

Hearing voices on deck, I arose from my short slumber and climbed the galley steps to survey the weather. Reaching the Port of Miami around 3 A.M., the vivid blue violet skyline blended with the tangerine hues of the early morning. The city lights of the high-rises glistened ever bright and crisp. What a glorious time to reach land! In the face of adversity, hope had remained true.

I cherish the friends I made, marvel at how many lives were saved, and well remember our laughter—and especially the teamwork of my fellow sailors in this piece of nautical history termed Tropical Storm Jerry.

A Faux Pas in Paradise

by
Mimi Peel Roughton

My husband, Lucien, is outgoing and talkative—he truly enjoys meeting people. But he can be impulsive and doesn't always think before he speaks. It's all part of his considerable charm.

To celebrate our fifth anniversary of the night we met, which was on January 6th—the day Christians celebrate the Epiphany—I booked us a tropical getaway. This would be the first Caribbean cruise for either of us. We agreed that our five years together had been the best years of our lives, and love, indeed, was more wonderful the second time around, so we decided to splurge. The small, luxurious ship carried just 225 passengers.

We left frozen North Carolina for warm, sunny San Juan, Puerto Rico, with our Christmas tree still trimmed—we're Episcopalians and take full advantage of the 12 days of Christmas. We arrived in San Juan too late on the night of the sixth to enjoy the charming Latino custom of *Dia de Reyes*—King's Day. Other folks staying at our hotel told us at breakfast how darling the children had been the night before, coming around to receive gifts. I'd not thought about that when making our plans and I could've kicked myself—I should've planned to explore Old San Juan before rather than after the cruise. Lucien said, "Let it go, Mimi."

Later that morning we stepped outside our hotel, laden down with my bags—many, large and heavy. I'd vastly over packed, but I liked to have options. I envied women who could wear just one pair of fine gold loops, a simple necklace and a wedding ring for an entire vacation. But I'm not one of them—I'd brought practically my whole jewelry case. Lucien had packed quite a large bag himself, those being the days when nobody at the airport really cared how much your luggage weighed.

We tried to figure out how to catch a bus down to the dock, which was visible at the bottom of the hill. But without Spanish, and so weighted down with bags, we weren't having much luck.

"I give UP!" Lucien yelled when yet another bus rumbled by the bus stop without stopping. "Goddammit, it's right down there," he said, pointing down the steep hill covered with warehouses and seemingly miles of steps. "Let's just WALK."

I refused, and he headed off, pulling his suitcase across the road. Furious, I hailed a taxi a few minutes later, and was napping in our glamorous stateroom when Lucien huffed in—in a foul mood—45 minutes later. I was angry that he'd left me, he was exhausted from schlepping bags, and we didn't speak.

But an hour's sleep did us wonders. I woke to his brown eyes and mischievous smile. "Look what comes with our stateroom!" he said, holding up a giant bottle of Mount Gay dark rum. I giggled and kissed him, and we were back on track, ready for fun. We spent our first afternoon onboard drinking the wonderfully earthy Barbadian rum mixed with pineapple juice, exploring the ship and sizing up our fellow travelers.

By dinnertime we were in exceptionally good spirits. We'd dressed a bit for dinner, but hung back a moment upon entering the dining room—as first timers, we weren't sure where to sit. Almost immediately a genial New Yorker—let's call him Bob—asked us to join him, his wife and their travel companions.

We sat down and ordered white wine—we always start with white, then switch to red. The fact that wine with dinner was included in the price of the cruise was one of the reasons I'd picked this particular cruise line.

Characteristically, Lucien started casting around for conversation. One thing about Lucien, he's not afraid of taking risks in conversation—a trait that often charms people. What he said was probably the first thought that crossed his mind.

"You know, Bob, I don't usually notice other men's hair, but when we saw you embarking today, I was so impressed with your full head of hair I thought you must be wearing a rug."

I looked up from my shrimp cocktail, alarmed at the subject matter. Bob's friendly face had lost all expression. Lucien blithely went on, "But later when I saw you by the pool, I could tell it was your natural hair. Damn, I'd give anything to have that much hair!"

The table had gone quiet. A look of horror bloomed on Lucien's face as we both leaned in closer and realized that (*Oh, shit!*) the man *was* wearing a toupee. While Lucien started backpedaling like mad, I stood up abruptly, excused myself and made for the ladies' room. I'd had enough of his impulsiveness for one day.

"I mean, I mean . . . ," I heard Lucien stammer before I escaped earshot. Mortified, I applied lipstick and wondered how we could possibly avoid these folks on such a little ship for a whole week.

Somehow we did manage to keep our distance. At our multi-cappuccino breakfasts and at dinner, we'd notice where they were sitting and head in the opposite direction. One night in the karaoke bar, Lucien enjoyed a triumph that felt at least a little redemptive—his rendition of *Strangers in the Night* was so spot-on that at first everyone thought Sinatra himself was singing. But before we entered the bar that night, we scanned the crowd to make sure *they* weren't in attendance.

On the days we went ashore—to St. Bart's where Lucien got to drive a small car fast around dangerous curves along gorgeous cliffs—European-style, and we hung out in bathing suits at our first nude beach, to Martinique where I tried on dozens of duty-free perfumes, and Lucien bought me Givenchy's smooth-smelling *Amarige D'Amour*—we always made sure there were several people in line between us and Bob.

On those occasions we couldn't avoid Bob, et al., we'd apply smiles, flutter a quick wave, and then turn back to each other as if in deep conversation.

At night in bed in our elegant, wood-paneled stateroom, at least half-drunk from free wine and liquor, we'd remember the incident and feel horrified all over again. Then one of us would giggle, the other would guffaw. I'd bury my face in Lucien's chest and we'd laugh until our tears wet the fine linen sheets and pillowcases.

Top: Lucien and Mimi before departing on their January 2004 Caribbean cruise.

Bottom: 2012 cruise on the Turkish seas, where Mimi and Lucien renewed their wedding vows.

A Touch of Luck

by
Nelson O. Ottenhausen

During January 2007, while sailing the Caribbean on a Carnival Cruise Lines' ship out of Miami, I got lucky and won a few things. No, I didn't gamble, but instead I attended art auctions during the travel time at sea. Each session I attended, I received a ticket for a drawing—the prize, a work of art.

At the first auction, I won a seriolithograph of a painting done by the artist Emile Bellet entitled *D'or et de Reve*, Gold and Dream, appraised at $595. At the second session, I won another one of Emile Bellet's seriolithographs, also appraised at $595.

By the fifth session I had won three more seriolithographs by other artists—Linda Le Kinff, Itzchak Tarkay and Anatole Krasnyansky—all valued at $595.

While returning to my stateroom after that fifth auction, I spotted a jewelry vendor outside his shop, promoting a drawing with gold-plated jewelry pieces as prizes. First prize would be a necklace and bracelet set, second prize, a necklace and third prize, a single bracelet.

I got in line and before I received my ticket, a woman behind me asked, "Aren't you the one who's been winning all those paintings at the art auctions?"

Turning around, I replied, "Yes, I am."

She smiled, placed her hand on my shoulder and rubbed it a few times, saying, "It's for good luck."

"I hope it works and you win something," I said.

After giving a short description of his wares, the vendor began the drawing for the three prizes.

As he started to pull out the first ticket from a large glass bowl, the woman behind me moaned, "Oh God, please."

The man read the winning ticket's series of numbers and when he finished, I heard a loud shriek and then felt a couple of light backslaps. The same woman who had rubbed my shoulder pushed me aside and hurried up to claim her winnings. She returned after getting her prize and gave me a quick hug, and then left, all without saying a word.

Then I heard the next series of numbers being called for the second drawing—my number. As I went toward the front of the crowd to get my prize, no less than five elderly ladies touched me and smiled as I passed them. They too had attended the art auctions and had seen me win the five pieces of artwork. They also had noticed the woman behind me rub my shoulder for good luck, so they thought they'd give it a try. Later during the cruise, I found out that two of the ladies won jewelry prizes at other drawings.

By the end of the cruise, I'd won more artwork and more jewelry. I had eight seriolithographs, one necklace and two bracelets. But my luck hadn't run its full course just yet.

On the last day at sea, I came in late to the last art auction already in progress, but the drawing for the seriolithograph had not been conducted yet. As I entered the room, an associate of the auctioneer handed me a ticket. I then went to my usual table and sat down. Looking around, I estimated the audience to be about 45 to 50 people.

The auctioneer had seen me come in and as I was taking my chair, he announced over the public address system, "Well, folks, guess who just walked in? Mr. Ottenhausen has set a record in winning eight pieces of artwork on this cruise. Hell, we might just as well give him the seriolithograph now and save us the trouble of going through the motions of conducting a drawing."

The audience applauded. Then 15 minutes later, after the auctioneer had sold the last work of art, he announced the drawing and drew the winning number—mine.

Murder on the Good Ship Lollipopooza

by
Cappy Hall Rearick

Two years ago, I was a passenger on the Good Ship Lolli-popooza, navigated by the intrepid Captain Crunch who refused to make port because he didn't want to get his ship dirty. So we kept sailing and sailing while chefs kept cooking and cooking and sympathetic bartenders kept pouring and pouring.

One night after two—OK, make it three—martinis, as I waited for the elevator to arrive, I happened to overhear a conversation of an elderly couple. I didn't mean to eavesdrop, but, hey, I'm a writer. It's what I do. You've been warned.

He said, "Murder can always be made to look like suicide. It's easy."

My ears perked up. My martini legs wobbled while I leaned closer so I could hear more. Being a writer does not mean I have a lick of sense.

I stepped on the elevator with them but stood near the emergency button in case I needed to make a fast getaway from Medicare Bonnie and Clyde.

He said, "If we're going to do it tonight, we should get out of these clothes first."

She gave him a look. "You're right. I wouldn't want to mess up my good shoes."

He said, "Not to mention that pretty dress you're wearing."

OMG, I thought.

I moved even closer to the big red emergency button.

Gazing at them, I thought they looked like grandparents in a Norman Rockwell Thanksgiving painting. I could see him decked out in a suit worn only twice a year, his holiday bow tie slightly catawampus. I imagined him sharpening the knife and carving the turkey, while she, smiling sweetly, waited at his side, wearing a holiday apron and holding a bowl of yams with those little miniature marshmallows on top.

I cleared my throat.

"Pardon me," I said. They looked up as though seeing me for the first time.

"I didn't mean to listen in on your conversation, but I think it's only fair to tell you that I'm a newspaper columnist and I might have . . . *might* have overheard the word *murder* as we were getting on the elevator. I heard wrong. Right?"

They looked me in the face and didn't say a word. They didn't even blink!

I got very up close and personal with the big red button.

I was jabbering, but eventually it hit a home run with them because they tore their eyes away from mine, looked at each other and burst out laughing. I, on the other hand, was not amused. I was freakin' freaked out.

"I'm just a small-time columnist," I said, defensively. "I don't write for a biggie newspaper like *The New York Times* or the *Daily News*, so whatever you're planning to do or not do, you have nothing to worry about. Your secret is safe with me."

They kept staring at me like I was the one about to get my picture put up in post offices all over the country.

"You should know that writers make a habit of eavesdropping because we live very dull lives so we have to steal experiences from other people. Not nice married couples like you, though. I'm rambling, aren't I? Let's just forget everything I said, OK? Oh, please, can I get off the elevator now?"

She giggled.

He said, "We're not married. At least not to each other."

She said, "He's better than a husband. A great lover. Aren't you, sweetie?"

TMI alert!

He turned to her and said tenderly, "Well, I wouldn't call you a slouch in that department."

OMG. Will this elevator never stop?

She eyeballed me. "We've embarrassed you. Well, take it from me, cupcake, you gotta make hay while the sun shines."

He laughed. "And make Betty while Fred's moon shines." Then they both laughed till tears rolled down their cheeks. "She's Betty—I'm Fred. Get it?"

I so wanted off that freaking elevator.

Betty leaned over, nuzzled Fred right in front of me, big as you please. "Oh, Fred, you're gonna kill me yet, you know that?"

Holy homicide! The doors opened and I galloped out

of there faster than the racehorse named *I'll Have Another.* When I looked back at them, they were still checking me out and laughing. I shivered.

Fred called out to me. "Hey you, Ms. Brenda Starr! Meet us up on Deck 12 at midnight for the Murder Mystery Game Finale. It's been going on all week, but with your imagination, you'll catch up in no time."

At least that's what I *thought* I heard him say.

CHAPTER FOUR

Expect the Unexpected

You just never know what will happen . . .

One Night in Paris

by
Eve Gaal

My parents meant well. They had this amazing idea that our family of five could pile into Mom's used Lincoln, travel across the United States during the world's biggest energy crisis, board us and the Lincoln onto a ship bound for Europe, and then use our family car to sightsee around Europe, thus saving on railway fare. Stranger still was the notion that once we were done, we would travel back the same way we came, home to California.

Now I'm no harsh critic of the hand that fed me, and I always found it odd that Beverly D'Angelo and Chevy Chase were chosen to portray my parents in the *European Vacation* movie, but all I can say at this point is thank goodness we didn't go to Stonehenge. Fortunately, for all involved it was a memorable experience full of exciting hair-raising experiences that will supply me with writing material for decades.

I'm recalling famed French singer Edith Piaf's sweet but sorrowful voice and our one night in Paris. The City of Light, gorgeous and lovely with pastry shops, strolling musicians, croissants and baguettes, all clamoring for the tourist dollar near romantic cafés—unless, of course, you're like the Griswalds in that movie, roaming around the international expressway that swoops you around and around Paris like virgins around a maypole. In fact, the large phallic object in this case was the Eiffel Tower.

Meanwhile, we were five hungry American tourists who didn't speak a word of French, wondering where to exit with our monstrous yellow car. The map was out and Mom was pointing and oohing and ahhing until we finally drove into the darkest part of the rainy city. And it wasn't pretty. Besides seeing graffiti everywhere, we spied very sexy ladies leaning against the buildings in the rain. The public facilities were flooded for some reason, reminding me of my freshman textbook account of vermin infestation and black plague. Wasn't that in the Middle Ages?

The year was 1974. I was 16 years old and it was springtime in Paris. And it could only get better. We drove by the street sign that said "Louvre" because our giant gas guzzler would never fit onto the Rue de Whatever. My father paused, wondering which way to turn, finally parking in underground metered parking at the City Centre.

We went to find a room for the night. As soon as the reservation agent saw our group in our rumpled, wrinkled clothing, he informed us politely that there was a conference in town and that the hotel rooms were sold out. Determined, my mother went next door to an even higher-class hotel.

I sighed, anticipating the luxurious ornate and lovely room awaiting my family. Combing my hair in front of the wall of mirrors next to the reception area, I applied lip gloss and tried to look sophisticated. Again, we were told about the conference. I wondered if it was code for "We don't rent to strange Americans." Honestly, looking back on our ragtag group and knowing a little more about the haughty French, I couldn't really blame them for having higher standards.

Finally, of course, my mother found a place. The man smiled, twisting his waxed moustache. She smiled back and asked him the price. Now leering, his eyes zoomed in and ogled her décolletage. We were dripping wet, like the rats floating around the edge of the Seine heading for those public facilities.

Remember, this was back when Motel 6 charged only $6 a night. My very beautiful and adorable mother was perfectly willing to go up to $100 for a room in Paris, France. But this was pre-Euro, and even though Mom was exceptionally good at math, the $500 conversion was way beyond her practical sensibilities and what she was willing to pay. Grabbing my hand, she pulled me and my siblings back to the parking garage where Dad waited in the car, snoozing with our luggage.

"We have to move the car," she said, tapping him on the shoulder.

"OK, but why?" My father started the engine and we exited back out into the rain.

"The parking in this garage is only for hotel guests, and it is not free. I tried four different places and they said there's a convention."

"But it's getting late. Don't you think we need to go to sleep?" he asked, yawning.

I watched the lights of Paris disappear from the sky behind the Eiffel Tower. And then somewhere amid the chaos and the pouring rain that night, we slept—in our Lincoln Continental—dreaming of the warm American hospitality at Motel 6.

A Bawdy Night at Tahoe

by
Carolyn T. Johnson

Something about a truck driver wearing red sequins just didn't compute. Could my eyes be playing tricks on me? I wondered to myself, trying to make sense of what was happening.

It all started out as an innocent family weekend trip with my husband, stepson and daughter-in-law. What better place to indulge in a little skiing, gambling and dining than in Lake Tahoe, where the lights stay on all night long? Rumor had it they pumped pure oxygen into the casinos to enhance that wide-awake feeling.

The first day of our trip, the skiing conditions were perfect—sunny, with just enough powder to leave a wake. That night at dinner we feasted on filet mignon, lobster tails and several bottles of California's finest. I cautioned my young daughter-in-law about the revue we were scheduled to attend later that evening.

"I'm not sure if you know what you are in for. I remember my virgin voyage to Nevada years ago. I bought a ticket for a show thinking it was all about the dancing and headdresses. I nearly fell out of my chair when the first pair of mammaries popped up on the stage," I shared with her. "But in no time, the scenery was brimming with leggy women wearing nothing but head feathers, G-strings and teeny tiny party hats to cover what the law wouldn't allow."

I felt good about giving my daughter-in-law fair warning as we moseyed on over to the Horizon Theater to check out Gypsy Rose Lee and the Divas of the Carnival Cabaret. We settled into our reserved front row seats in the cozy arena. The waitress brought our cocktails right away, and then Gypsy sashayed out from behind the velvet curtain. She wore a long, red, sequined, spaghetti-strapped evening gown, with a sparkly gold and crimson hat and matching gold *lamé* wrap. She was kind of pretty in a matriarchal way, as long as you didn't look too close. Tons of black eyeliner caked her eyelids that struggled to support her bevy of false lashes. Heavy rouge emphasized her sharp cheekbones and set off her ruby-red lips.

She grabbed the microphone to welcome everyone to the show, but when she spoke, her voice belted out like a New Jersey truck driver who'd just given up smoking. She was, as she so proudly proceeded to confess, a transvestite. So much for the warning.

During the evening, Gypsy welcomed her cast of lookalike stars onto the stage, one by one. They all sang very convincing renditions of hit songs, looking and sounding close to the real thing, even though they were not women by birth.

Dolly Parton practically burst out of her skin-tight turquoise dress with each breath. Diana Ross sang while decadently dragging her white fur along behind her. Barbara Eden's getup flashed back to an old *I Dream of Jeannie* rerun. Marilyn Monroe wore her infamous V-neck, blow-my-skirt-up dress. Selena strutted her Tejano self around, looking vampy in her big silver hoops. Whitney Houston beamed like her early happy gospel singer self, and even Bette Midler looked convincing with her blond locks.

All the performers were so into character that we sang right along with them to most of the songs. Dolly even bounced out into the audience and buried my husband's shiny pate in her man-boob cleavage. I threw my hands in the air swaying to the Motown tune when Diana's perfectly manicured hand reached out to touch mine. They were having so much fun that they volunteered to stick around for photos with us afterward.

What I first thought was a fiasco ended up being a fantastic burlesque show. Maybe it was because we weren't expecting chicks-with-sticks, or maybe because they were really talented entertainers. But nonetheless, on this trip, we had a ball . . . no pun intended.

Inner Ear, Outer Limits

by
Frank Ramirez

"Have you read most of those books?" That's what people ask when they see a portion of my library. And I answer, "Mostly."

I do read a lot, but some books are reference works, like biblical commentaries, which I consult rather than devour. You don't read those cover to cover. And then there are those I've owned for years, even decades, and just never got around to reading yet. They're on my to-do list.

That's why recently, as I packed for a flight to visit my folks out west, I looked for one of those neglected reading to-do's to scratch off my list. Air travel is a great time for reading. You arrive really early to get through security, after which you're stuck at your gate with nothing to do until boarding starts.

Then there's the flight itself, hours of sitting all cramped with total strangers on each side while the guy ahead of you leans back for a nap and puts his headrest practically in your lap. Then a couple more hours at your layover to change planes, more waiting, maybe three or four more hours of flying, and finally landing.

There's not much to do but read. And that's why picking a good book is so important. It either better be very exciting so you don't notice how long you're spending in airports and in the air, or really boring so you'll fall asleep, making time pass even more quickly.

I decided to take a dusty old paperback of *The Once and Future King* that I'd purchased while I was in high school back in the late 1960s. I must have bought it after seeing the old Disney film *The Sword in the Stone*, which is one of the four novels that make up the book. The book cost all of a dollar when it was printed, but that was a lot back when most books cost only a quarter. It was published after a few incidents in the story were cobbled together for the musical *Camelot*. Richard Burton and a very young Julie Andrews graced the cover of that old red paperback.

Forty years later and I'd never got past the first page. It seemed time, time to cross *The Once and Future King* off my to-do list. How was it? I have to say I enjoyed what I read on that flight. It's the King Arthur story, after all. What's not to like? I was just finishing the first part—*The Sword in the Stone*—when the flight began its descent into Dulles Airport near Washington, DC.

I noticed I was perspiring just a little on the nape of my neck. And behind my ears. My forehead, too. All I'd eaten were some almonds earlier in the flight—no food service in the air, remember? —and they were starting to sit funny in my tummy.

The plane jerked up and down. The plane swung from side to side.

I looked up.

I closed my book.

I closed my eyes.

I'm always open to new experiences. *Wow*, I thought. *This must be what people feel like who get airsick. Of course since I don't get airsick, there's no problem. I'll just not read for a minute or two . . .*

Hmmmm . . .

I've flown many times, and I always enjoy it. I've been through some rough weather, too, real bumps in the road, but it never bothered me.

Suddenly, I asked myself, *Don't they have airsick bags in the seat pocket in front of me?* Not that I needed one, but it wouldn't hurt to find it.

Well, you don't need the details. Let's just say that I have never been in a plane that rocked and rolled like this one. At one point there was a bolt of lightning, our lights flashed off and on, and I'd swear sparks flew out. I felt like I was in a cement mixer. We twisted and turned.

I could hear people throwing up all around me. It would have bothered me more, except they were all probably imitating me. I realized I had started it. I don't usually think of myself as a trendsetter, but for once I was ahead of the curve.

You may have heard the old joke where someone tells an airsick passenger, "Don't worry. Nobody's ever died of airsickness." To which he replies, "Don't tell me that. The hope of dying was the only thing keeping me alive."

It didn't sound so funny anymore. I just hoped we'd touch down soon. But we didn't.

The pilot announced the weather was too rough to land, so he took us back up to a higher altitude and flew around the city to try another angle. That meant we had a short break, and then it started all over as we descended into the weather once more. I was vaguely aware that someone in the row behind me was handing me an extra airsick bag. Good thing—I filled that one, too. And once again I wasn't alone.

When the plane finally touched down, everyone cheered. I took some deep breaths, and then staggered out of the plane, wobbled through the terminal, waited on the curb half an hour for my shuttle, the rain falling all around me, then drove two-and-a-half hours home in a driving rainstorm.

Drat. I had really wanted to finish *The Once and Future King*, but I began to wonder if I could ever pick up that book again. For a couple of days I couldn't read anyway. I mostly sat because the house wouldn't stand still. Everything kept spinning. But I recovered.

As it turned out, a week later I made an unexpected flight out west and back to lead a funeral. The flight was gentle. I opened the book. I read the book. I finished the book. It was a great book! Why had I waited so long to read it? And finally, I crossed it off my to-do list.

That felt good.

Almost as good as I felt when I made sure, before going to the airport, to pack a heavy-duty airsick bag of my own devising.

Thank heavens I didn't need it.

The Pits of Hell

of
Dellani Oakes

I've never been to the pits of hell, but I have been to Miami.

It all started one summer in the early 1990s when my sister-in-law invited us down to Miami for an overnight visit. I packed the kids in the car and headed south on Interstate 95. Confident I could find the way even without a map, I made the four-hour drive with my son in the backseat and my 9-year-old daughter riding shotgun.

While the children visited with their cousins, I talked to my brother-in-law about the return trip home.

"Traffic gets pretty heavy by 8 o'clock. You'll want to be on the road no later than 7:30."

We weren't. It was one of those mornings where I couldn't get my children up and moving for anything. Finally, well after 8 o'clock, we got on the road and headed out of town. We hit a snarl of traffic less than two miles from their home, and crawled along for over an hour. Once clear of that, we made good time and flew up the road—until somewhere south of Titusville.

Flashing lights ahead warned of some calamity. We were directed off the road at the nearest exit, which branched a short way from the interstate. I was trying to figure out which way to go when the skies let loose a deluge. By the time my windshield cleared, I was committed to a road and headed off, hoping to find my way to U.S. Route 1.

After a time, it became quite obvious that we were no-where near US-1 or I-95. Heading east, we could see the launch tower for Cape Canaveral. I was totally lost. As this was before GPS or cellphones, I had to find somewhere to ask directions. There were no gas stations, convenience stores or other signs of civilization until we were about half way to the Cape. I spotted a rundown bar and made my way there.

From the outside, it looked like a dive. The wooden walls were warped with sun, rain and wind. The roof was ready to collapse. Beer signs flickered in the windows. I didn't dare leave my children in the car, nor did I want to bring them into a place that looked like it hosted biker gangs and ax murderers, but I had little choice. There was literally nothing else around.

Girding up my loins and putting on my brave face, I got the kids out of the car and headed to the door. As we approached our destination, a car full of men drove up. They hopped out, dressed in suits and ties, looking for all the world like a bunch of rocket scientists and NASA executives on lunch break. I caught up with them at the door to the bar.

"Excuse me. Can you tell me how to get to US-1?"

"You sure you don't want to go up I-95?"

"No, there was an accident or something there. I'd rather avoid that."

The best-dressed executive stepped forward, motioning to his friend. "Bill, you want to take this one? After all, you're the rocket scientist."

Bill stepped forward, smiling broadly. I was given directions by a bona fide rocket scientist. I thanked him and we piled back into the car. I drove to US-1, following his impeccable directions, and turned north. A few miles up the road, we saw evidence of the thunderstorm's passing. It must have been accompanied by high winds that we'd avoided by going to the Cape. Downed branches littered the road, making driving difficult.

A few miles farther up the road, there were more emergency lights and we spotted a car overturned in a ditch. No one could have survived that crash. Traumatized, I stopped at a Burger King and ordered lunch for us. While the children ate and played on the playground, I sat with a cup of coffee and tried to stop shaking.

By the time we got home, it was nearly dinner time. I collapsed on the couch and told my husband what I'd been through on our drive home. He clicked on the TV and went to fix supper. I lay there watching the news until something caught my eye.

"Police led in high-speed chase." I sat up, turning up the volume. I listened to the report about a bank robbery and apparent kidnapping which had taken place that day in Port St. Lucie, south of Cocoa Beach. The bank robber had escaped and they thought he had his girlfriend as a hostage. He led police on a high-speed chase up I-95, stopping on an overpass around Titusville. He held a gun to his head, but officers still thought he had his girlfriend in the car. They blocked off the highway, diverting traffic to US-1. Eventually, the robber shot himself, ending the standoff.

The broadcast continued. A squall had passed through Titusville accompanied by a small tornado. A handful of people were killed, including two who died when their car overturned in a ditch. They showed footage of the scene—the car we'd driven by lay abandoned in the ditch.

The shakes came back stronger than ever and I thanked God and my angels for protecting us. Had we gotten an earlier start in Miami, we would have been on I-95 when the gunman barreled through. If I hadn't missed that turn to US-1, we would have been on the road when the tornado passed. What started out as a pain-in-the-butt day turned out to be a lifesaver. Never again would I curse and scream about being stuck in traffic during a trip. Instead, I'm thankful for the delays, figuring it keeps me from something far worse.

No, I've never been to the pits of hell, but I have been to Miami.

International House of Band-Aids

by
Cappy Hall Rearick

While on vacation in Temecula, California with my husband, Babe, we ate lunch, shopped on the cobblestone streets of Old Town, and did some wine tasting. We toasted each other with thimbles full of very young red wine while the entire Northeast Coast—where we lived—schlepped around in knee-deep snow.

Driving back to our daughter's, who lived in this wonderful California desert area, I was hit with a severe headache that worsened with each bump in the road. Every throb sent rejection signals to my stomach for what it had been subjected to for the past four hours. By the time we got home, I was sick enough to beg Babe to call 911.

Remember what your mother told you about wearing good underwear in case you're in a wreck? Here's a new one: "Wear good underwear in case you are loaded onto a gurney by four young uncoordinated medics. You don't want to be sporting a raggedy-ass bra." Mine was a bra on which I had cleverly sewed two shabby shoulder pads.

Down the steps and into the ambulance we flew, four paramedics and me in my bra with tacky shoulder pads and old undies. I looked down to see that I was half naked.

"Babe!" I cried. "How could you let me expose myself to God and everybody in Los Angeles?"

Holding my head in my hands, I tried not to scream each time we hit a pothole. The driver was either paid by the hour or he had a little drug business in the front seat. It took 30 minutes to drive five freaking miles. My vote was drugs—nothing else made sense.

Once in the ER, I was put on a gurney that felt as if it had been made out of a tree stump, and I was told not to move. Every now and then a doctor with a thick foreign accent would stick his nose into my cubicle. "Zo zowwy. Much beezy tonight. Code blues ebbywares. Be back in few meenits."

To which I'd quickly respond, "An aspirin, an aspirin! My Queendom for an aspirin!"

Babe didn't hear me. He was too busy pacing a ditch in the floor.

After a while, another foreign-speaking medical person popped in to say, "We do CT scan now." Before I could think to reason why, he whisked me off, bumpity-bump, to a room where I became the brunt of some serious blonde jokes.

I figured the medic must have been an East Indian Buddhist because he asked me the same question over and over. "Zen? Zen?" I would reply, "No, E-PIS-CO-PA-LIAN." I found out later that he was asking me WHEN I had injured my head.

The medic whirled the CT scan thingie around my head ad nauseum. Begging for mercy, I was bumped back to the cubicle where, by that time, Babe appeared to be pacing on his knees. Either that or my brain was gone and the East Indian Buddhist fellow missed seeing that in the CT scan.

At the sixth hour of my ER adventure, the sweet-talking Dr. Obi bin Doolittle came in and popped me with a slug shot of morphine that in a scant second had me believing I had sprouted wings and could actually use them. As I prepared for takeoff, the good doctor ignored my don't-wear-in-case-you're-in-an-accident undies and slam-dunked a needle into my rear end.

"Now ve muus kep you obernight so ve kon vach you."

"Why? What's wrong with me?" I could no longer feel my nose and my eyes were jumping like I'd just spent the night in Starbucks. Yikes. I wasn't supposed to die of a terminal headache.

I tried to focus on the doc's face, but it was tough since my eyes were boogying at their first prom. I said, "Hey, Doc, thank you, but no thank you. You have fixed me up all better and, like ol' James Brown, I'm feeling good! Head no ache, stomach no throw up. Me go home now." When in Rome.

As it turned out, my dreaded demise was a migraine brought on by an allergic reaction to nitrates in the thimbles full of wine I had chug-a-lugged. The determined doctor wanted to make sure I didn't become a morphine monkey junkie on his watch, so my tush stayed planted in a real hospital bed for the rest of the night where every 30 minutes a young nurse sobered me up long enough to take my blood pressure and my temperature.

The nurse spoke *poco* English, which made me fear I had

crossed over the border at one point during my stay at the International House of Band-Aids. The only person whose spoken word I understood was an African-American nurse who—thank you, Jesus—hailed from the Deep South where I was born and raised. We high-fived in the same language.

Eight hours and $4,000 later, I was discharged, albeit reeling from the staggering cost of my short confinement, which almost caused another migraine. Armed with Ibuprofen and a good martini, I could have spent some of my vacation suffering at the Ritz-Carlton—and it would have been a lot cheaper. But then, I couldn't have checked out of the Ritz newly fluent in seven different languages!

Dig a Hole

by

J.D. Riso

We trudged up the long dirt driveway at Ralf's Place in Wewak. All I could think of was washing the travel scum off my body. We'd made it through four days on Papua New Guinea's Upper Sepik. The guides had told us that we were only the second group of solo female travelers to ever visit there. Somewhere under my fatigue and disgust was pride.

"I bet we reek," I said to Maya.

"I hope there aren't any other travelers here," she answered. "And I don't care what Ralf says, I'm wearing shorts around his guesthouse. I'm sick of wearing jeans in this heat."

We rounded the last bend. Ralf, a gaunt, gristly whipcord of a man, waved listlessly as we walked up to the weather-beaten house.

"So, I see you have made it," he said in his heavy German accent. "There are others here now. You will take the room on the right this time." He turned and walked over to the shed without another glance at us.

Under my breath I said in a mock German accent, "And you will like it."

We giggled. Pain shot through my gut—a toxic gas-filled balloon. I winced.

"Still no luck, eh?" Maya asked, a sympathetic look on her face.

I shook my head as we walked into the house. A young couple was seated at the table, sorting through their documents. We introduced ourselves. They were British expats who were traveling through PNG before returning home. He was pasty-skinned and reticent. Her lilac perfume hung in the dense, humid air. I stood for a moment and let it envelop me.

Maya and I walked into our room. We put our backpacks on the free beds.

"You go first," Maya said. "You look like you're about to keel over."

The cement-floored, cold-water shower made me tear up with joy. Cobwebs adorned the ceiling corners, but the spiders were only as big as my thumb. I soaped up and rinsed off, running a hand over my swollen stomach. I looked like I was six months pregnant. *There's no way I could put those jeans back on,* I thought to myself.

Suddenly, something shifted in my abdomen. My intestines twisted and knotted like some vindictive fetus. I kneaded and prodded, gritting my teeth against the pain, hoping to relieve some of the pressure. I squatted and spread my legs like a sumo wrestler and bore down. After a few moments I gave up.

It was about as futile as trying to extract an air bubble from a block of ice without smashing it to bits. My bowels had turned to cement.

I slipped into a sleeveless knee-length sundress, another no-no, according to Ralf. Showing shoulders or thighs was a legitimate excuse for rape in PNG. Looked like I'd be hanging around his place until we headed for the airport the next night.

A group of three Australian men joined the British couple. Maya got up from the table and headed for the shower. A tall, beefy blond was in the middle of telling a story: "So, John decides he has to take a leak while we're at the market. He walks around the side of a shed. Suddenly, some guy runs behind him with a machete. We panicked, but turns out the guy was running after someone else."

I laughed with everyone, though I gasped with pain. The British woman looked at me for a long moment. The others didn't seem to notice.

"So how was it out there?" the blond guy asked me.

"Hot, smelly, miserable," I said, and laughed in spite of the discomfort. It's already a funny memory. Such is the power of soap and clean clothes. "Big, hairy spiders everywhere. Rats screeching and running over our mosquito nets at night. The guide cooked us rotten fish one night for dinner."

The guys shot me condescending looks that said "sissy girl."

I shrugged. *Let them find out for themselves.* There was a reason why hardly any women—or foreigners—had been to the Upper Sepik. *I bet they'd be reduced to tears in less than five days.*

The pain in my gut intensified. I had a hard time catching my breath. I got up and walked outside to the outhouse. The stench made me swoon. I could hear maggots feasting on the filth at the bottom of the hole. It was a wet, meaty sound, like oozing mud. I put my face in my hands and tried not to cry.

The British woman approached me. "How many days has it been?"

"Over a week, since before we went up the river. I thought it would be better out there, but the outhouses were infested with huge spiders."

I started to shake at the memory of squatting over a hole in the dark hut. The spiders—all of them as big as baseball mitts—became visible as my eyes adjusted to the dark. They were everywhere I looked—on the wall just inches from my face, hanging from the ceiling, on the seat itself (thank you, Mom, for teaching me never to sit on public toilets), and on the door frame where I was about to put my hand. It was like something out of a 1960s' B horror film: "Just when you thought it was safe to take a dump, your safe haven turns into *The Outhouse from Hell!*

With this scenario suddenly seared in my mind, I ran out of the hut with my pants around my ankles, screaming and slapping my hair and clothes. The villagers laughed at me. They ate the damn things when they couldn't find anything else.

"There's no way I'm going in there!" I said, pointing to the outhouse.

She put her hand on my shoulder and nodded her head knowingly. "No one can relax in such filthy circumstances. I learned while traveling through India that it's just better to dig a hole."

I grimaced.

The woman continued. "Dear, this is no time to be a prude. Look where you are. This place is a dump. Ralf is too damn cheap to buy lime for his outhouse. He can get away with it because he has the only guesthouse in Wewak. Just go out back to the jungle and dig yourself a hole."

I looked toward the narrow trail leading through the dense growth. She gave me a gentle push and walked back into the house.

I waddled up the trail until I found a small clearing. I brushed the fallen foliage away with my foot, and then hiked my dress up and squatted. From this position, I saw a plump green snake slither off languidly into the deep brush. I tensed up and another spasm moved through my gut. With a heavy sigh, I stood up, arranged my clothes, and waddled back down to the guesthouse, resigned to the fact that true relief would not come until I was back in civilization.

I'm Ready for My Close-Up

by

Erik Bundy

I'd been in Bordeaux, France, only three jetlagged hours and already I was lost. Behind me loomed the magnificent St. André's Cathedral where cultured Eleanor of Aquitaine had wed monkish Louis VII in 1137, a few years before they departed on a disastrous Crusade. I had no idea how to return to Merignac, the bedroom community with my landlady's house on a quiet bystreet. Only a few people strolled through the cathedral's square. I noticed two tram stations, but didn't know which line to take or even how to buy a ticket.

Three hours earlier, my landlady had met me at the regional airport, had accepted the box of French chocolates I bought for her in Paris, then had taken me to the room where I would stay for the coming six weeks. She also had given me a sheet of paper that I stuffed into my shirt pocket while we talked.

After I'd unpacked, she asked if I'd like to see Bordeaux's

Old Town. Sunday afternoon it would be quiet and uncrowd-
ed—just right for exploring. Still manic with cross-Atlantic
jet lag, I thought a walk would calm me. She drove me to
St. André's Cathedral in the heart of historic Bordeaux and
pulled over to the curb. When she asked me something, not
understanding her French, I nodded politely. She waited until I realized that I was expected to get out of her small white
Citroen. I did, but instead of parking nearby, she drove off.
Something had been lost in translation. And now something
else was lost—me.

Well, I'd flown here to immerse myself in another culture
and to learn French. Now retired, I'd planned to pursue un-
fulfilled dreams, leave the cocoon of small-town living behind
and spread my wings. I wished for quiet adventure, and maybe
my wish had come true.

Since I was here, why not explore the area? Normally,
famous monuments interested me less than the common history and culture of where I stood at the moment. St. André's
Cathedral was an exception, mainly because of my interest in
the fascinating Eleanor of Aquitaine, a traveler herself. I also
wanted to walk along nearby Rue Sainte-Catherine, a main
pedestrian thoroughfare even in the times of togas and Roman sandals. Besides, walking might calm me and fool me into
believing I was in complete control of this situation.

First, though, I'd scan the map at the nearest tram stop
and fix on a strategy for getting back to my room. Being lost
always took more time than I thought. And it would be a *faux
pas* to miss the first supper my landlady cooked for me.

I must have looked lost because two young men in jeans

and baseball caps walked up to me. I almost touched my bill-fold to make sure it was safe. How much would they ask for? When I didn't understand their French, one of them introduced himself to me in English.

"Would you act in a movie we are making?" Aram asked. If nothing else, their approach was novel and amusing.

"Sorry," I said, "but I don't speak any French at all."

"This is not a problem," Aram said. "Our film is in English for to have more international appeal. We require an older gentleman to play the role of a blind man talking to a younger man. The old man is also a famous film director."

What was their game? I wondered. *Did they expect to con me into giving them money by asking me to subsidize their film? Or would they simply lead me into an alley and mug me? Or could this be a legitimate offer?* Small adventures sometimes pattered up to me on sly little mouse feet.

When I didn't decline outright, Aram became more confident. "We are from Armenia and have a small production company," he told me. "We are making an art film."

I refrained from asking if that meant I had to take my clothes off.

"It is unfortunate," he went on, "but we will not be able to pay you. Our budget is very small."

For me, a country is not its map or its territory, but its people. Leaving the cocoon meant engaging with the local people, and this had the added advantage of introducing me to an unexpected part of Bordeaux's populace, the immigrant Armenian subgroup. So I agreed.

Hakob took a phone photo of me for publicity, and we

exchanged email addresses so they could send me the script. I was still wary, but I could think of no way to tap into my bank account through my email address. Would my publicity photo show up somewhere on a fake passport?

We agreed to meet in this same place Wednesday and shook hands. Feeling somewhat blessed by fate, I walked over to St. Andrés Cathedral. As I pushed my way through one of its high wooden doors, I met a blind man coming out and remembered I was soon to play one. So I stayed on the square a few minutes to watch him. His manner of handling himself and competence amazed me. It was something I would never have noticed if I'd not met Aram and Hakob.

Later at a tram station, I found all the routes were color-coded and had no trouble buying a ticket from a vending machine and purple-lining my way back to Merignac. Once there, though, I wandered lost on deserted streets in search of my landlady's neighborhood. Was the address perhaps on the piece of paper I'd stuffed in my shirt pocket? Yes, it was, along with detailed directions on how to find her house.

Aram sent me the script the following day. I wrote back to say that it read like an English translation of a French text. The natural American speech rhythms were stilted. But he was in luck. A writer, I'd gladly revise the entire script for them. Aram emailed me to say they were delighted. Fate had brought us together.

So after my morning language classes, I rewrote the script. Besides being a blind retired American movie director, my character was also a ghost. His retirement had been more final than I'd expected.

Now when I walked around vibrant Bordeaux, I watched blind people handle themselves in public. Their white plastic canes had tiny balls on one end. They rolled these across the pavement in wide arcs in front of them instead of tapping these white sticks as I'd expected.

Aram and Hakob were surprised to learn I was 15 years younger than they'd believed. This was, I decided, because of my white hair and the fact that youth often errs when judging older people's age. No way could my actual appearance have anything to do with their miscalculation.

On Wednesday, Aram met me at the cathedral and escorted me to San Bruno, Bordeaux's grand cemetery. Here the aristocracy, crowded out of the San Bruno Cathedral's churchyard by their predecessors, had built numerous tombs and filigreed family chapels for themselves.

While Aram talked with a cemetery official, I walked around the tomb of a deceased sea captain. On it stood hollow-eyed Death, lichen-covered, with a sharp scythe in one skeletal hand. Again I congratulated myself. Had I not accepted this movie role, I would never have seen this cemetery, this awe-inspiring outdoor museum of French architecture.

Hakob and his three young assistants arrived with all of the filming equipment. It was 90 degrees and cloudless. We filmed for five hours among the recumbent crowd marked only by names and dates. I became sunburned, something everyone else noticed but me. At one point, Hakob and Aram discussed using a camera filter but they decided instead to edit out my growing redness later. Ghosts don't get sunburned, and my face was bright enough to guide Santa Claus's sleigh.

While most of the scenes shot that afternoon were fine, traffic noise around the cemetery and a helicopter flying over-head required us to redo the dialogue. We agreed to meet at Aram and Hakob's apartment the following evening.

Stepping behind the scenes into their lives was as interest-ing as the filming. They lived in a vibrant immigrant section of Bordeaux. From their open window on the ground floor, I watched Armenians and Moroccans and Africans parade by on a brick street bustling with life. We redubbed the film's dia-logue, and then drank a robust Saint-Émilion wine that tasted slightly of licorice while they told me some of their homeland's 6,000-year-old history.

Hakob came from a quaint Armenian village within sight of grand, snow-capped Mount Ararat. If I wished to visit his ancient country, he said, I only had to tell him, and I'd never need a hotel. His friends and relatives were scattered every-where there.

My six weeks in France seemed to pass in the blink of an eye. I spent much of it in the friendly company of my well-met young friends. They made my trip not a vacation from life but an engage-ment of it. In getting lost, I'd found a new role to play.

So now I'm saving to wing my way to Armenia. Visiting this ancient land where silk and spice caravans once plodded adds a tingle of possible new adventures to my future. My new friends may offer me another movie role while I'm there. After all, I'm ready for my close-up and my deserved acclaim as an international film star.

(see photos, next page)

Top: Erik on the quay in Bordeaux.

Bottom: Death atop a shipbuilder's tomb

Planes, Trains & Automobiles

It's the journey that counts.

War in the Skies

by
Stacey Gustafson

If you're like me, you hate to fly these days. Flying has become tortuous since X-ray body scans, flight cancellations, smaller seats and lost luggage. We travelers are sometimes treated worse than cargo.

But there are strategies to employ in order to survive flying. Southwest Airlines offers an open-seating policy where customers can grab any unclaimed seat. On a recent flight from San Jose to St. Louis, I hatched a scheme. I waited for my number to be called at the terminal, rushed to the first available empty row and grabbed an aisle seat. Then I set a trap like a spider to solicit a seatmate.

Anyone skinny, without kids or a large handbag, and who appeared germ free met my prerequisites. I spotted a possibility and announced to her in a loud voice, "Excuse me. Would you like to sit here?"

"Oh, thanks. How thoughtful," she said.

More like self-serving.

But on airlines with assigned seating, your seatmate is a crapshoot. Take a recent Delta flight. Without checking my ticket, I was confident I was in the right row and grabbed a prized aisle seat. I stowed my books, attached the seat belt and waited. And watched. A rather portly man came barreling down the aisle, eyeing my area.

Oh, God, please no. Just keep walking, I thought. Let's just get it out here—one size seat does not fit all. He lumbered by.

I survived the next wave of crying kids, sneezing teenagers and businessmen with briefcases. A slim, petite woman smiled in my direction. *Jackpot, come on over.* She fumbled to check her ticket and said, "You're in my seat." I checked and rechecked my ticket. She checked hers again. *Damn, I had the wrong seat!*

I returned to the main aisle and moved down a few rows. Like Dwayne "The Rock" Johnson, a man over 6'4" and 250 lbs. was in the aisle seat of my row. I squeezed past Big Guy, climbed over his huge shoes, oversized coat, bulging briefcase and big bag of greasy takeout food. I avoided eye contact out of pure irritation.

Then the flight attendant announced, "Put away all electronics. Buckle your seat belt."

Mr. Big dug around his seat searching for the belt, knocking me in the chest with his mammoth elbow. "Sorry. Can't find the darn seatbelt."

A few more jabs to my ribs and the search was over. I glanced out the corner of my eye to watch him buckle in, no seatbelt extender necessary. Whoosh, like a can of biscuits, flesh exploded over and under the armrest and filled in all available spaces.

After removing his shoes and stuffing the extra blanket under my footrest, he asked, "Honey, could you please turn on the overhead light?"

That was his opportunity to snatch my armrest. My skinny arms were no match for his muscular, oversized appendages. I tried to ignore my discomfort and took a short nap. When I awoke, I discovered my tray table down, crowded with a cup of water, a can of soda, a coffee mug with the contents half finished, and *The New York Times*. An iPad was squeezed to the side, the cord dangling across my lap.

I let out a sigh and fought to keep my mouth shut. Despite its size, the tiny bathroom would be a welcomed reprieve from the cramped setting.

"I need to go," I said, and rolled my eyes as he removed all his items from my tray table. Then he stood and let me by.

Over the loudspeaker, the flight attendant said, "Due to turbulence, you'll need to return to your seat, please."

You've got to be kidding.

In my hurry to be reseated, Big Guy moved to the middle seat. Despite his "nice" gesture, sitting in the aisle seat proved as bad. He leaned on me the rest of the flight, bending my spine like a case of scoliosis. I was so far into the aisle my head got clubbed by the drink cart.

Soon our captain announced, "Prepare for landing."

Once on the ground, I gave Big Guy a smooch on the lips. Then I whispered in my husband's ear, "Thanks for the terrific vacation," squeezed his arm and motioned for our kids in another row to wait for us at the exit.

Maybe next time I can be upgraded to first class.

Stacey naps while "Big Guy" takes over her space.

Surrealism Express

by
Nancy Davis Kho

When I was 20, I went to an exhibit at the Museum of Modern Art. A sophomore at college where I studied business, the depth of my art knowledge was confined to the great works I'd memorized by playing "Masterpiece" in middle school. But this exhibit of the great masters of Viennese Art—Klimt, Kokoschka, Schiele—made my heart thump. Beauty and melancholy in equal measure, the stories behind each soulful subject begging to be understood.

Standing in MOMA on that snowy, New York City winter day, I resolved to apply for a semester abroad in Vienna. I wanted to learn more about the rich Secessionist art movement, to really understand the history that produced these designs in art and architecture, so was thrilled when I got accepted to a six-month program there.

As is often the case with travel, the lessons I learned weren't exactly the ones I anticipated.

I arrived in Vienna in January, amid one of the worst snowstorms in recorded history, and immediately learned that I should have packed better boots. I learned what it feels like to be a foreigner instead of a native, how the spoken Viennese accent has virtually nothing to do with the High German I'd studied for eight years, and how to play my part in the traditional mincing dance of polite subservience that characterizes a purchase transaction in an Austrian shop—where, by the way, it's the customer, not the clerk, who is subservient.

Of course, I did fill up on the art, buying cheap student passes to museums and palaces where I could sit and soak up the work that I loved so much. But by the time spring break rolled around in April, I was ready for a change of scenery and champing at the bit to see more of Europe.

My best friend from home was in Europe that semester too, so we hatched a plan to meet in Florence to explore it and Venice together. Unfortunately, when I arrived at our rickety *pensione,* I received a message that my friend was stranded on a Greek island, thanks to a strike by Hellenic boat operators. The best she could do was to fly out to Vienna and meet me a week later.

My reflexive reaction was disappointment. The sensible thing would be to return to Vienna and wait for my friend. I moped around the piazza near my hotel and ate heartbreakingly good pizza and pitied myself until it dawned on me—I could still explore Italy as I'd planned. I'd just have to do it alone.

I spent the next five days walking all over Florence, then,

a short train trip later, I arrived in Venice, with only my guide-book for a companion. I struck up conversations with people with whom I never would have spoken if I weren't alone. As the days passed, I grew increasingly confident in my abilities as a solo traveler.

On the last day of the trip, I got captivated by the canals and bridges of Venice. By the time I made it to the train station, there was only one option left to make it back before classes started—the night train.

Horror stories about Italian night trains were common currency among American exchange students in the 1980s—perhaps they still are. We all believed, with full faith, that if you fell asleep in your Italian train compartment, roving bands of thieves would pipe sleeping gas into the air vent and help themselves to the contents of your overstuffed American back-pack. A casual observer of night trains in Italy during that era would have seen vast numbers of wide-eyed American teen-agers, slurping oily European coffee and clutching their back-packs with both arms and legs while glancing furtively up and down the train corridor.

But I was now a five-day-seasoned solo traveler. Plus, I had no choice. So I boarded a car packed with Italians, qui-etly opening their picnic dinners or their evening newspapers. Sure, they looked innocent. I gripped my backpack until my knuckles bulged.

I was seated across from a slightly older Italian man who was a dead ringer for American actor Rick Moranis. One glance at my luggage death grip and he started practicing his conversational English. When we'd covered my hometown, his hometown and the weather, he asked, "Where are you headed?"

My answer caused Italian Rick Moranis to jump up and down, point at the door, and shout at me in Italian. Finally he calmed down enough to stutter in English, "You are on the wrong train! This will unhook! You must go to the front!"

I'd made the rookie European traveler error of getting on a train car that would be uncoupled at the next station, and my new Italian friend was going to make sure that I got myself up to the proper train car during the short stop, even if it killed one of us.

As the train slowed, he hoisted me into my backpack and shoved me out of the compartment, yelling, "You must run to the front of the train!" The train had not actually stopped when he popped me out the door with a thrust to the back-pack. I bicycled my legs in front of me and prayed to find pur-chase when I landed, and when I did, I pivoted and sprinted as fast as I could toward the front of the train.

But I was able to dig deep and find an even faster stride when I glanced back to see Italian Rick Moranis running four steps behind me, now yelling, "I LOVE YOU! I LOVE YOU!"

I was so glad to see the beckoning open door of the third car of the train that I hurled myself through the opening with-out looking around first. I was just glad to be safely out of reach of a man who was, let's face it, a bit too quick to give his heart away. I stashed the backpack into a luggage rack, sat down and looked around.

That's when I realized I'd flung myself onto an Italian army troop train.

The only stories scarier to young American women in Europe than the "poison gas through the vent" fables were the "I was groped by ravenous young Italian men" variety. And now I was surrounded by tanned, dark-haired, black-eyed Italian men in uniforms, without a commanding officer or another woman in sight. What with my home peroxide treatments, I was a goner for sure. Why, God, did you make me a shade of fake blond reputed to be so captivating to Italian men?

Except the soldiers never once looked at me, for the entire hour we shared a train car. They stared moodily at their reflections in the window, or buffed their nails, or spoke in quiet voices among themselves. But not once did they look my way. Relief settled over me, followed inevitably by resentment, and then a vow to lay off the Viennese pastries for a couple of days when I made it back to Austria.

After the soldiers disembarked, I was left alone in the compartment. We'd pulled out of the station when a young woman walked past and glanced warily inside. She passed two or three more times before finally opening the door and sitting opposite me. The woman was dressed plainly and wore no makeup, but it couldn't disguise the fact that she was stunning, with clear blue eyes and a cascade of long brown hair. It didn't register with me right away that she had no luggage.

It took only a few moments before Lorena introduced herself and started telling me her story.

It seemed that Lorena was fleeing the country and her abusive boyfriend, who she said was connected to the Italian Mafia. Her safe haven was a convent just on the other side of the Austrian border from Italy, where she knew a nun who would take her in. Her plan was to live out her days safe from the mob as an Austrian nun—if only she could make it across the border. She carried neither passport nor money for the train ticket.

I was fascinated as Lorena's story unfolded, while the train chugged north to Austria and into the dark of night. I insisted she take some of my food, gave her some money, and strategized with her about what we would do when the Austrian border control officials boarded the train. In thanks, she broke open a small egg-shaped chocolate that comes with a cheapo plastic trinket inside, and insisted I keep the trinket, a neon green plastic pear, to remember her by. She ate the chocolate.

The train slowed in the inky darkness and finally stopped at the Austrian border. We could hear the border police moving slowly down the corridor, checking passports, and Lorena darted around the compartment like a cat in cage. But there was nowhere to hide. The Austrian officials opened our door, asked to see our passports, then summoned Italian police when Lorena failed to produce one. Politely but firmly, they asked Lorena to accompany them off the train. She looked at me mournfully, and I clutched the neon green plastic pear to my bosom, waving goodbye to the gorgeous nun on the lam.

By now it was the thickest, deepest part of the night. I sat alone in the compartment, thinking it might finally be safe to nod off.

But the door opened again and in walked two tall punks, each with a ceiling-scraping Mohawk—one green, one red—and face piercings, dressed in black leather, chains and spikes. Red glanced at the book that had sat open on my lap since the soldiers departed. It was in English.

"Are you American?" he asked.

Great. I steeled myself for the barrage of anti-American criticism that often followed my response to that question. Worse, it was the Reagan era and I shared a first name with the First Lady, which always drew snide commentary. I nodded slowly.

An enormous grin appeared on Red's face. "I love America! I've been to New York. I'd love to live there someday!" Green was similarly enthused: "We listen to American music all the time!" Ten minutes later, they'd spread out a particularly toothsome middle-of-the-night picnic on the seats between us, opened a bottle of wine, and we spent the rest of the trip to Vienna talking music, art and culture. When the train pulled into Vienna's central station, I got hugged so hard by Red and Green that they left spike marks in my forehead.

Here I was thinking I'd gone to Vienna to learn about the Viennese Secessionist art movement.

But what I really learned was Surrealism.

Venice

Moose Meadows Waterloo

by
Kayleen Reusser

The day my husband, John, had been looking forward to for months had finally arrived. After carefully studying the various options, he booked the two of us to fly with a private plane operator over Mount McKinley as part of our week-long 25th wedding anniversary trip to Alaska. Now that the day was finally here, he could hardly contain himself. He was giddy with delight during our drive to the operator's base.

I, on the other hand, dreaded the thought of climbing aboard the plane.

Many wives, I knew, would relish sharing such an experience with their husbands. The opportunity of seeing one of the most beautiful sites in North America could bond us together with memories to last a lifetime. But, if given a preference, I'd view the mighty mount from the ground.

It wasn't that I didn't respect the highest peak in North

America. We had taken family vacations to national parks and hiked with our children among many mountains.

It was flying in a small airplane that bothered me. More specifically, it was the *motion* of flying in a small airplane that bothered me.

Motion sickness was something I'd battled since childhood. It seemed to run in the family. Before each car trip, Mom used to place a clean, empty bucket in the back seat between my sister and me. The bucket usually didn't stay empty for long.

Small planes aren't the only things that caused me to lose my lunch. Roller coasters, bus rides and boats also did a number on my digestive tract. Thankfully, over the years I've learned some tricks to combat this tendency—sitting in the front seat of a vehicle helped, thus allowing cool air from the A/C to blow on me. But there was no front seat on the plane, so I decided to prepare for the two-hour plane ride with a trip to the pharmacy. Some old over-the-counter friends greeted me, as well as new medical acquaintances.

Motion sickness pills were as much a part of my growing-up years as the bucket in the back seat. Whenever Mom had had enough of the pukey smell in the car, she would give my sister and me a couple of motion sickness pills. Unfortunately, the pills worked so well that Sis and I would fall asleep before the car left the driveway and remain groggy the rest of the day.

But now I didn't want to ruin this special day by barfing or falling asleep. Besides, each seat on the plane cost $169. I swore to myself that for that price, I'd stay awake every minute and enjoy the trip, even if it killed me. I just didn't know how I'd do it.

When the pharmacist held out copper wristbands for me to examine, I nearly grabbed them out of his hand. "Position them over each wrist's pulse points," he said, showing me the proper location. "The copper helps maintain your equilibrium."

I wanted to tell him I had lost all my equilibrium in my mother's birth canal, but I kept silent. After all, who's to say these copper wristbands wouldn't work? They must have worked for somebody, or they wouldn't still make them, right?

With wristbands firmly in place and feeling newly confident, I smiled at Doyle, our pilot, as John introduced us. We learned that another couple would join us for the flight.

My smile slipped a little when Doyle handed me a clear, empty zipper-sealed bag. "Something for the trip," he said.

I thanked him, guessing John had mentioned my problem during a phone call. I placed the see-through bag on my lap under the two white barf bags I had taken from the much larger plane that had carried us to Alaska. Doyle's clear bag would be a last resort—who wanted to look at the contents of one's stomach anyway?

The pilot seated John and me behind him. The husband of the other couple sat in the front passenger seat, while his wife took the last available seat behind John. I thought about asking for the front seat, but I didn't want to be a problem, so I stayed quiet.

The first hour passed quietly as we flew over glaciers and mountain ranges. "We're lucky to have a clear day," Doyle told us through the headphones we each had donned. "McKinley should be out."

Since the mountain known alternately as Denali or "The

High One" is only visible one day out of three, we counted our blessings and took dozens of photos from the windows of the plane. The cool breeze from the vent felt good. As the minutes passed and the plane sailed along smoothly, I started to relax. By the time we started our return trip, I felt confident I'd make it through the rest of the flight with no mishap.

Then one of the passengers—I won't say who, but I'm married to him—asked the pilot to close the cold air vent, as it was drafty. I wanted to shout, "Don't you dare! I need that air!" But I kept silent, though I felt myself begin to sweat.

"Focus on a stationary object," the wristband instruction booklet had recommended. I stared at the horizon, trying not to think about my increasingly clammy hands and face.

About an hour and a half into the trip, Doyle pointed to something over the back of his right shoulder. "Oh, shoot. I forgot to show you all something," he said. He steeped the plane to make a 180-degree turn and I knew I was done.

I lost the battle over Moose Meadows. I used both airline bags, which was a surprise since I had eaten little for lunch. I never found out what Doyle wanted to show us over Moose Meadows. It could have been the Titanic perched on top of a glacier with Leonardo DiCaprio at the stern for all I cared.

When we landed, I crawled out and handed Doyle the two full barf bags. He looked surprised but didn't ask questions. I kept the clear bag for future use.

With my knees weak and throat scratchy, I wanted nothing more than to sit down and drink something. But John asked Doyle to take a photo of the two of us standing in front of the plane. I managed a weak smile while John held me steady. It was the trip of a lifetime for my husband, and I was glad he had enjoyed it.

As for me, I was thrilled to be back on the ground. As for the copper wristbands, they went in the first trash can I found. I'll stick with the pills, thank you very much.

Kayleen and John standing in front of their airplane, following the flight over Mount McKinley and Moose Meadows.

Corpus Christi Shrimp Run

by
John Reas

Ordinarily, it takes just over four hours to drive from Killeen, Texas to the sandy beaches of Corpus Christi. The distance on a Friday between Fort Hood—where we were stationed—and a great weekend in the sun and surf along the Gulf Coast totaled exactly 284 miles. We intended to take advantage of every second along the way.

Five of us set out that late July afternoon. Smack and Boss led the way in Smack's 1985 Toyota Celica Supra. Boss rode shotgun, while Slug, Trig and I followed behind in Slug's CJ-7. I was placed strategically next to the cooler in the back of the Jeep since, with the top down, I found that a steady supply of beer made the road trip that much more appealing.

Smack also had packed an empty cooler to haul back the shrimp we intended to pick up while in Corpus, because we knew the others in our battalion would never let us get away with returning without the means for a Sunday evening cookout.

"This is going to be great, guys!" I shouted to make myself heard above the wind, while Slug followed Smack onto Interstate 35. "We should be able to pull into Corpus by 9, drop off our stuff, and go hit the bars. Of course, some of us don't have to worry about reporting in to the wife back home."

Trig, the only married one among us, turned back to me, "Yeah, but at least I'm not like the rest of you losers who will spend the entire weekend making total jerks of yourselves trying to score, only to crash and burn like always. And besides, Maria knows we won't get in until late and doesn't expect me to call in when we get there."

Slug, our designated driver, eyed Trig's beer with longing. "And just how long has it taken you to finally get the kitchen pass, anyway? This is the fourth time we've make the shrimp run, and I think the only reason Maria finally released you was because she was sick and tired of your whining about missing out on a road trip with the boys. I'll take my chances at crash and burn. Beats the ball and chain you're wearing."

Trig snorted. "Yeah, we'll see who'll complain when I get back Sunday night to Maria, and the only thing you can claim to have scored will have been a load of fresh Gulf shrimp."

I knew better than that. Smack and I shared a townhouse in Killeen. He was the one single officer in the battalion who *never* had trouble picking up women. Many a Friday night, I'd come home from the Fort Hood Officers' Club to see discarded clothing and emptied wine bottles in the living room and hear telltale sounds emanating from his bedroom.

We made it to Corpus Christi and the naval air station

where we dropped off our bags at the Bachelor Officer Quarters, and then headed out to enjoy the nightlife. First stop was Snoopy's Pier off South Padre Island Drive, one of our favorite watering holes and home of some of the best grilled shrimp in Texas. We pulled in and headed to the back of the restaurant to catch the setting sun while we nursed Coronas.

"You know, guys, Lindsay's in town," I said.

"Lindsay who?" Smack's eyes lit up.

"An old friend from high school. She's a computer consultant and travels a lot, but I told her we were coming down, and she invited us to drop by her place tomorrow."

"And she has friends?" asked Slug.

"None who would be interested in you," chortled Boss. All of us had just seen *Top Gun* and were convinced that as Army officers, we were far superior to any Navy flyboys and certainly had more to offer to the women of Corpus than the aviators from the naval air station.

After Snoopy's, we ended up at Sharkey's Beach Club in Port Aransas. Finally, by 2 A.M., with none of us having any success with the young women we encountered, we stopped by the original Whataburger.

"JR, Lindsay needs to come up with some babes to hang out with us tomorrow night," Smack said, bummed that he'd not had his usual Friday night success.

"Well, I said we'd be by her place at 6. Just remember, she's an old friend from school, so don't you clowns act like you normally do," I warned.

We drove back to the BOQ and crashed. By the time we woke up and staggered out in the Saturday sun, it was nearly noon. We grabbed breakfast, and then headed to the beach where we joined a game of pickup volleyball. After an hour, our team lost a round, so we found ourselves on the sidelines as another team stepped up to the net. Trig decided to cool off in the sea.

Smack turned to Boss and said, "Look at Trig, all alone out there. Let's give him some company."

Boss laughed. "I'm with you!" Trig was wading near the shore when they grabbed him, and as the three struggled, Boss yanked off Trig's swimming trunks. The two culprits howled with laughter as they raced back to us, leaving Trig stranded in the surf.

Trig looked ticked, and it was hard to determine what was more red—his sunburnt shoulders or his face. By then, the small crowd around the volleyball net was looking to see what the commotion was all about. Smack and Boss laughed their asses off as they tossed the trunks next to our towels.

Trig finally yelled, "I'm coming out, and I don't care who looks!"

He stormed out of the water like a raging hippo and snatched up his trunks while the crowd scattered. He yanked them on before tackling Boss to the sand. Boss convulsed with laughter.

Smack approached with some beer as a peace offering. "Here, Trig. You really know how to make an impact with the ladies here on the beach!"

We glanced around and noticed two gorgeous, sunbathing brunettes laughing as well. Soon we edged our cooler closer to their blanket, as Smack started to make his move. The women were schoolteachers in their late 20s, down from San Antonio for the weekend.

The afternoon flew by, and soon I noticed that it was past 5. "Hey, we need to go pick up Lindsay." Smack wasn't eager to leave by then, but one of the teachers said, "Go ahead. Tell us where you'll be later tonight, and we'll meet up then." We agreed to meet back at Sharkey's around 9.

We found Lindsay with a frozen margarita, sunning herself by her apartment pool. "JR, it's good to see you again," she exclaimed, giving me a hug. "It's hard to believe it's been a year since I last saw you! And who are these hunks with you?"

"These are the boys from my unit. Trig's married and therefore harmless, and Slug is pretty decent, but you will want to be on full alert with Boss and Smack here. Especially Smack."

Smack gave Lindsay his best wolfish grin and said, "Any woman friend of JR's is definitely a friend of mine."

Lindsay rolled her eyes. "Well, I'm glad to meet ya'all. 'Bout time you came, 'cause I'm starving. Two of my girlfriends are meeting us at the Water Street Oyster Bar and are curious to see what a bunch of soldiers from Fort Hood look like. I told them that I know at least one of them has half a brain."

Slug chimed in. "Well, it can't be Trig, as he keeps losing his swimming trunks." That earned him a punch in the arm while Smack proceeded to recount the afternoon's activities.

Lindsay laughed. "JR, you should have warned me before you brought your zoo to town!"

When we got to the oyster bar, Lindsay's friends were already there. They had never been around anyone in the military before, despite the proximity of the naval air station.

Nonetheless, before too long, the eight of us were chatting like old friends. The beers were flowing by then, and when Smack shouted, "Let's split for Sharkey's!" a little too loudly, one of Lindsay's friends offered to drive. Smack gladly surrendered the keys to the Supra, and Boss jumped in the other car that Lindsay's friend, Sandra, had driven. The rest of us crowded back into Slug's Jeep.

Sharkey's was warming up when we arrived. And there, right on time, was the San Antonio twosome. Smack's eyes lit up as he grabbed one of the teachers by the waist and lead her to the dance floor. Before long, all of us were out there as the disc jockey spun Duran Duran and Phil Collins. The rest of the night, the 10 of us hopped from bar to bar, and somewhere along the way, we managed to lose one another. It was around 3 A.M. when Sandra and I noticed that we were alone.

"Where did everyone disappear to?" I asked.

"JR, I guess it's just you and me. It's a good thing I'm the designated driver, huh?" I wasn't sure if it was a good thing, since we'd been trading tequila shots, but she volunteered to take me back to the base. We managed to make our way back to the BOQ and stepped into the room that I was sharing with Smack. Only Smack wasn't there alone. Everyone else was there as well. Lindsay was snoring away in the corner, the two teachers were sprawled out on the bed, and the others were crashed on the floor around the room. Empty beer and wine bottles were scattered among the slumbering bodies.

Sandra took one look, nodded and passed out next to the door. I apparently followed suit, because the next thing I remembered was waking up with the rest of the walking dead well after noon. We all looked like road kill. Somewhat embarrassed, we said our goodbyes as we packed up. The five of us made the longest 284-mile drive home with the worse hangovers in the history of mankind.

A memorable road trip indeed—except we *forgot* the damned shrimp.

John at Fort Hood

When Pigs Fly

by
Mary-Lane Kamberg

"Should I get one of those surgical masks for my flight to Oklahoma?" I asked my daughter Becky, who had just returned from Arizona.

Swine flu dominated the news. On TV, people in airports wore masks. I was soon to fly from Kansas City to Oklahoma City for a conference. I worried about inhaling the other passengers' recycled air, including any flu germs they might carry. The plane I would be on traveled between Chicago and Houston and Houston was darn close to Mexico, where the outbreak began.

"There was a woman on our flight who was wearing one," Becky said. "You'll like this part: she was sitting in the third row, and there were four empty rows around her. Everyone thought she was sick and headed for the back."

"I'm going to buy a mask!" I said. Extra space for the price of a 99-cent mask would be better than a first-class upgrade! I'd be delighted with a whole row to myself.

I was flying a first-come-first-choose-your-seat airline. As a frequent flyer, I had developed several methods to discourage passengers from sitting next to me—reading a book, pretending to sleep, spreading out my purse and jacket onto extra seats—all with mixed results. Wearing a surgical mask could make others look for ways to avoid me.

On the day of my flight, I boarded the plane and settled into an aisle seat. I slipped on the surgical mask I bought at the pharmacy. It covered my nose, mouth and the hair on my chinny-chin-chin. People behind me in line kept on going when they got to my row. They avoided looking at me, like children whose mothers taught them not to stare.

When everyone was seated, I not only had a whole row to myself, but no one sat in the row across the aisle either. I moved to the middle seat and hogged the whole row. I spread out my purse, book, magazines, bottled water and a bag of pretzels. My space soon looked like a pig sty.

I settled back and became aware of my breathing. I exhaled and moist heat filled the mask. Without warning, my heart rate accelerated. I gasped for air the same way I had during my first scuba lesson, after I had donned the diving mask and mouthpiece and the instructor told me to put my face in the water. As I had then, I calmed myself using a deep-breathing technique I learned in my yoga class.

Around me people sneezed, coughed and sniffled. I smiled inside my mask. After landing, I exited and tossed the mask in the trash.

At the conference banquet, I entertained participants at my table, talking about my successful strategy. "From now on," I said. "I'm going to wear a surgical mask every time I fly."

When I checked in for my return flight, I verified that the flight had enough empty seats for me again to have my own row. I boarded the plane, took an aisle seat and put on a new mask. I left my seatbelt unbuckled so I could slide into the middle seat for takeoff. Again, other passengers glanced at me and then looked away with well-practiced, don't-stare ease.

Boarding was almost complete when a porky woman wearing a pearl necklace appeared in the doorway. She made eye contact with me and beamed.

I opened my book and pretended to read.

She forged ahead down the aisle, stopped in front of me, and nodded toward the window seat. "Do you mind if I sit there?"

I'd rather kiss a pig, I thought. I stood and let her sit in my row.

"I was afraid I'd be the only one." She reached into her silk purse, withdrew her own surgical mask and smiled at me, her new best friend.

I cried wee, wee, wee all the way home.

Only in Texas

by
Kathleene S. Baker

He's simply a wannabe! I'm talking about my husband, Jerry, who would have swapped jobs with Charles Kuralt in the blink of an eye. I doubt Jerry ever missed an episode of *On the Road with Charles Kuralt*.

I admit the show was enjoyable, especially for those of us living in big cities. We often forget about the marvelous back roads, quaint small towns and beautiful scenery while we fly down freeways at breakneck speed to reach our destinations as quickly as humanly possible.

Jerry is in La-La-Land when driving those old back roads, two-lane highways, farm-to-market roads, and he does just that when given the chance. Stopping at mom-and-pop cafés, fruit stands and simply visiting with local folk always sends him home with a lively story or two.

Unfortunately, getting lost happens all too frequently

and usually in areas with no cellphone towers for miles. As he wanders about aimlessly on his travels, Jerry never knows what he'll encounter.

Once he stopped at an old, overgrown country cemetery. Weeds were thigh-high, yet he forged his way among headstones, which leaned in all directions, some crumbling and many illegible, as he looked for family members who had lived in that area. In the distance he heard barking, but assumed the dogs belonged to a nearby farm. As the sounds intensified, he took notice and began to look about. Suddenly, he realized a pack of wild dogs was headed right for him. He took off, and while stumbling over dead tree limbs, one new shoe took flight. A lucky grab saved the pair. He made it to his car just in the nick of time—and with the seat of his pants still intact!

Another lively adventure involved rounding up a herd of cattle. The wayward bovine had broken through a fence and their owner was in hot pursuit, chugging down the rough gravel road on his tractor, for he'd just unsaddled and put up his horse for the evening.

Jerry was cruising 'round the bend of that very road, singing *On the Road Again* along with Willie Nelson. The frantic cattle owner saw him coming, pulled into the center of the road, waved him over and asked for help. That day, a city slicker driving a Lexus and a seasoned rancher on his tractor actually managed to round up an entire herd and drive them back into the pasture.

Even in the middle of no-man's land, Jerry finds action during his Texas travels. While driving between Idalou (pop. 2,157) and Lorenzo (pop. 1,372), he noticed a lone building smack dab in the middle of nowhere. Surrounded by cotton fields and apple orchards, the adjacent parking lot was jam-packed with vehicles. Noticing what appeared to be a gift shop of sorts, with a sign that read "Apple Country," he pulled in and parked.

Jerry sauntered inside, scrutinized the various jams, jellies and such for sale, all the while chatting with an employee. "Where are all the folks who belong to that throng of autos?" he inquired, since he was the only customer in the shop. The sales lady explained that the Red Hatters were having a meeting in the back room.

Within seconds, a petite Red Hatter sneaked up behind Jerry, grabbed his arm and chirped, "I heard you askin' about us. Well, ya know this is a rural area, so our chapter is made up of ladies from small towns all 'round the county."

Jerry was not only startled, but at a loss for words. He didn't know what a Red Hatter was, and he'd certainly never seen one. He gawked at her wild red hat and finally mumbled something along the lines of, "Is this meetin' for fun, or is something illegal going on here?"

The Red Hatter giggled, her eyes twinkled and she knew she'd found some unexpected entertainment to jazz up their meeting. She grabbed Jerry by the hand and dragged him toward the back. "Come along now, son. I just can't wait for all the girls to meet ya!"

Being a gentleman, Jerry couldn't scuffle with the tiny gal, so he allowed her to pull and tug until they entered a room in the back. He did a double-take, for he found a room teeming with women in wacky red hats and purple clothing. "Ladies, ladies, this man is from Dallas and wanted to say 'hi' to y'all." The group waved and squealed. Red Hatters definitely are not the shy type!

Little did they know, but Jerry isn't the shy type either—he rather likes women, and especially feisty senior citizens. "Don't pay any attention to me—this sexy lady just kidnapped me on the jelly aisle!" Another round of laughter erupted, along with more waving, clapping and giggles. He told them his name, that he'd been out their way on business travel, and wooed them with, "Looking out there at all you beautiful ladies makes me feel like I must have died and gone to heaven—and this has got to be recess!"

Later that evening, Jerry barreled through our front door and began yammering about the Red Hatters, although he still had no idea who or what they were.

"Jerry, I've mentioned Hatters to you before. They're senior ladies with chapters all over the country. Their signature colors are red and purple and they do know how to have a good time," I explained. He didn't remember my telling him.

But Jerry's enthusiasm said it all. Happening upon, and being abducted by a lively Red Hatter, had made his day. Hopefully it spiced up their day, as well. I doubt those jovial little gals expect to see Jerry again, but I feel certain they will. He travels that route several times a year calling on clients, and he'll be keeping an eye on the parking area at Apple Country when he goes on his next road trip. And, masculine reasoning somehow left Jerry convinced that he was bestowed an honorary membership that afternoon when, in actuality, he was simply abducted by a witty Red Hatter in her seventies.

I say more power to the Red Hatters. Maybe they can keep Jerry in check during his travels, because obviously I sure in the heck can't!

We Didn't Take Any Pictures

by
Al Batt

My wife, the Queen B, and I had always wanted to see the Grand Canyon. I wanted to see a mile-deep gorge, 4- to 18-miles wide, and 217 miles long. A hole that big approaches the size of the potholes we get each spring where we live. I wanted to see something that would make my problems seem miniscule whenever I found myself in a hole. The Queen B said she wanted to see something that was even bigger than my mouth. And even though the Grand Canyon wasn't on our bucket list, it might have been had I not loaned our bucket to my brother-in-law to use as a seat for ice fishing.

I suggested to my wife that if we really wanted to see the Grand Canyon, it might be a good idea to go to Arizona, since that was the main gateway point to the national park. My wife could sense that I had done a lot of research in this area, so she agreed with me. I wasn't surprised. She had agreed with me once before. It was when I asked her to marry me.

We made plans to visit Arizona. I thought the best method would be to travel from Minnesota in a southwesterly direction. I also felt that if we were going to fly, an airline should be involved. I had to go to Phoenix anyway for some business doings and planned to combine work with a vacation with my lovely bride. The Queen B agreed and the next thing I knew, we were in Phoenix.

While in Phoenix, we did many fun things, including splurging on a hot air balloon ride across the desert, a delightful flight at a cost made reasonable by me providing much of the hot air. The name of the hot air balloon we flew in—the Hindenburg—did supply some uneasy moments. We rode in a basket, standing up in it like two drumsticks at a picnic. We watched a couple of other balloons bump into one another and enjoyed the argument that ensued between the pilots of the two. We floated high and free for a couple of hours, watching a van below struggle to keep up with us. The van was there to pick us up once we landed, but it was limited to travel via roads, while we traveled "as the crow flies." We landed in the desert, were dragged through a congregation of cacti, and then like good Minnesotans, we had breakfast.

At breakfast we talked of how time was getting away from us on our vacation and with my business obligations, how it was going to be impossible for us to drive to the Grand Canyon. It was right then and there that I made an executive decision—with my wife's permission, of course. We located an airline in Phoenix that flew small planes down into the Grand Canyon. I called them and the lady on the other end of the line described the flight "as more fun than an adult should be allowed to have."

I flagged down a taxi, the driver of which immediately took us to the wrong airport. Realizing his error and knowing what time we needed to be on the plane, he drove at an extremely high rate of speed to the correct airport. I didn't mind him driving down the sidewalk, and I loved it when he slowed to 100 mph for turns. I concealed my nervous anxiety by screaming in terror. I secretly wished I had brought a change of underwear. I made up my mind that I was going wherever the taxi was headed. I knew the flight had to be better than our taxi ride.

I was wrong.

The Queen B and I boarded a tiny plane with room for seven people, including the pilot. My wife took a seat in the back with four other intrepid travelers and I seated myself in the co-pilot's seat and tried to talk the pilot into letting me fly. We took off at about half the speed of the taxi. The plane was very noisy, but we were enjoying the flight. The scenery was breathtaking.

I found myself watching a little red plane flying close to us as we neared the Canyon. I had the time as the pilot had already stopped talking to me. I was watching this little red plane when, all of a sudden, it began to bounce up and down as if it were a basketball being dribbled by LeBron James. The plane was experiencing hot air thermals. I remember thinking, *I'm glad that's not us.*

It soon became us. We bounced as if our bodies had no bones.

Airsickness bags were put to good use. We flew down into the Grand Canyon. I saw the Grand Canyon. I think. We didn't take any pictures.

If you ever want to fly down into the Grand Canyon, I'd advise you to get the stomach flu instead. It's a lot cheaper and you get the same result.

Al didn't take any pictures.

Alaska or Bust

by
Arthur Bowler

"Let's drive to Alaska!"

That was the rallying cry of our family in the summer of 1963. Never mind the enormous distance between our home in Massachusetts and the 49th state. Never mind that a station wagon would be piled high with four kids, a dog and two parents, and that comfort meant something like having had a cold shower within the last few days. We had survived previous road trips all over the North American continent. Would we survive this one? One day we were not sure our sister would.

We planned a five-week trip, packed our car and tent trailer and headed off. The routine consisted of driving during the day and visiting local sights, pitching the tent trailer at night, and preparing meals outdoors over a gas cooker. It was not always easy for one teenage sister among three raucous, younger brothers, cooped up for weeks in a station wagon. As we three boys played and marvelled at the landscape and tourist attractions, our big sister was usually occupied with her copy of *Gone with the Wind*. There she sat, turning pages, occasionally looking up through sunglasses and responding to her younger siblings' excitement with a cool, "Marrrr-velous, guys."

We made good progress, driving through the U.S. and Canada until we reached the beginning of the legendary 1,523 mile long "Alcan," or Alaska Highway in Dawson Creek, British Columbia. Today the highway is paved, but in 1963 it was a rugged dirt road, quite unlike any highway we had ever seen in New England. We forged onward, slowly, until one afternoon when we almost lost our sister in Yukon Territory, a mountainous region with 0.17 residents per square mile. Somewhere in the middle of nowhere, we had stopped to get gas and visit the restroom.

Barrelling down the bumpy highway again after about 15 minutes, one of my brothers suddenly blurted out, "Where's Ann?" We looked at each other in stunned silence. We had forgotten our sister! We boys responded in rapid fire:

"She'll hate us!"

"She'll be cold!"

"She doesn't even have her book!"

The dog whined.

Our parents kept their anxiety to themselves. Was our pretty brunette teenager being propositioned by a French-speaking lumberjack? Was she furious at us? What would they think of this crazy reverend's family at the gas station? Long before the days of cellphones, our only recourse was to hurry back down the dusty highway as quickly as possible and hope for the best. When we returned, we found her sitting on a log, completely at ease, while we all sweated anxiously.

"Ann, we're sorry!" my mother called out through the open window before the car even came to a stop. "Are you all right? Are you angry?" We all watched and waited for her response—heads, hands and paws sticking out of car windows.

"I'm fine," she replied nonchalantly, glancing sideways. Then she turned to all of us, smiled beneath her sunglasses and added coolly, "I knew you'd be back."

And that must be one of the most fundamental principles of a successful family: the knowledge that mistakes will be made, but love will smooth over the bumps along the way, whether driving the Alcan or navigating the ups and downs of life.

We never actually made it all the way to Alaska, but we hardly went bust. Somewhere on the celebrated highway, after several flat tires, we decided that the trip was a bit too rough. As a family, however, we more than made it. We survived and grew closer, and today when we siblings come together, we still smile and remember our sister's famous words: "I knew you'd be back."

Yes, it's a thing called love, and it's as big as the Yukon Territory.

Rules of the Road

by

Dahlynn McKowen

As full-time, award-winning travel writers, my husband, Ken, and I have been all over the world and have experienced many happenings and surprises during our adventures.

Once I was serenaded in Italian by a toothless old man in Verona, Italy—the home of Romeo and Juliet—all because I was a blonde from California. I learned to snorkel in Honduras, drank the best cup of coffee in Munich, Germany, and kept a straight face in customs while declaring an antique Asian opium pipe when returning from Canada. I was spirited into and then won a tequila drinking contest in Mexico. I floated across beautiful, rock-studded Ha Long Bay, located on the border of Vietnam and China, in a dragon boat where I was served the best french fries ever!

And I'll never forget a thrilling 4-wheel drive trip over an 11,000-foot mountain in Telluride, Colorado, with the late General H. Norman Schwarzkopf at the wheel of his Chevy

Tahoe. He said not to worry, as the Secret Service had eyes on him at all times. Shortly after, Ken and I traveled to Costa Rica to visit dear friends Eldon and Janis Dale—who both have stories in this book—and shared the General's unforgettable trip with them. Eldon decided to one-up the General and took the four of us in his 4-wheel-drive Land Cruiser up and over a volcano. Eldon succeeded in scaring the crap out of me, and when we finally reached our destination—a macadamia nut plantation—I insisted he drive us home on the paved highway around the volcano. And he did. Smart man.

My most memorable trip though happened in Belize. Located on the Caribbean coast, with Mexico to the north and Guatemala to the west and south, this small country has the lowest population density in Central America. The locals are proud of their colonial heritage and are especially appreciative of tourists, with tourism generating much of the country's revenue.

Ken and I were traveling with many friends, all of whom were much more adventurous than me. The entire group decided they wanted to go on an exciting cave-tubing trip— floating on inner-tubes through dark caves, over waterfalls, and through God knows what, with only a headlamp for light. I balked. I'm not a fan of water adventure, so I opted to take a mellow boat ride through the mangroves, followed by a bus trip into Belize City to tour the Museum of Belize. My curiosity about seeing the museum was because it was the country's prison from 1857 to 2002, and we had written about prisons all over the world, from Alcatraz to the Hanoi Hilton. Plus, it was 2004 and chances were good that the new museum hadn't had much media coverage back in the U.S., so I wanted to take advantage of this possible freelance writing opportunity.

I kissed my hubby goodbye and took off with the other tour group for my anticipated boring and safe day. The boat ride was fun, but uneventful. It was mid-day, hot and humid, and the wildlife not abundant, with the exception of a few crocodiles sunning themselves on the bank.

At the end of the boat journey, our group of 30 passengers transferred to a luxury tour bus, all thankful for the air conditioning and ice-cold bottled water handed to us when we boarded. Our guide—Jorge—talked about the cultural history of Belize, as the bus whisked us through the countryside on the way to the museum. I learned that the country's official language was English, it was the only country in the region that was once part of the British Empire, and that it had gained its independence in 1992. For a country that was once a Maya civilization, its quest for sovereignty was to be admired and honored.

At least that is what I thought as I listened to Jorge talk. Many of the "Ugly Americans," who were sitting near the back of the bus, were just that—ugly. That's how we U.S. citizens are referred to in other countries when we display poor manners. The Ugly Americans on this trip rudely and very loudly carried on their own conversations, ignoring Jorge's historical and entertaining tour information. Several of us asked them to be quiet, to no avail. Finally, Jorge gave up and sat down.

Approaching Belize City brought a cheer from those idiots in the back. But what I noticed was that the bus driver wasn't slowing down as we were coming up on traffic and pedestrians.

I was sitting on the driver's side of the bus, about 10 rows back. He's going a little fast, I thought. Then the bus made a right-hand turn onto a busy street and clipped a horse-drawn service cart. "Hey! You hit that guy!" yelled an Ugly American woman. Jorge and the bus driver ignored her. We could see in that flash of a moment that the damage was minimal. But the cart's driver was a little upset, raising his hands into the air.

"Yo, driver. You need to go back there. You hit him!" yelled an Ugly American man this time, who turned out to be the gal's husband.

The bus driver responded with, "He was in my way. I had the right of way." I smiled to myself. Having traveled all over, I understood that the laws of the U.S. aren't the same laws in foreign countries. For example, in Costa Rica, if you leave absolutely anything in plain view in a parked car—from a blanket to a pen to a bottle of water—you are inviting another to break into your locked car and help themselves. The thief is not prosecuted. The same goes in some Asian countries: if a thief can see something in your home, and you don't lock your doors, it's an open invitation to take the item. That's why large, life-like dog statues are the rage in these countries—they are placed inside a home to scare off any potential thieves.

Nearing the town center, the bus driver slowed a little, but not by much. I half thought that maybe he was having a ball scaring the Ugly Americans. My mind jumped to the 1994 movie Speed, starring Sandra Bullock and Keanu Reeves, where a bus can't slow down because a bomb—planted courtesy of villain Dennis Hopper—would detonate and blow the bus and its occupants to smithereens.

The giant luxury tour bus weaved and darted and whizzed by everyone, with near misses here and there. The back of the bus grew very quiet, and I heard some "We're going to die" sobbing, but I was loving every minute of it. Boring trip, my foot! This is going to make a great story!

Once downtown, the road turned into a one-way street, with cars parked on both sides. Next to the parked cars were raised sidewalks and many colonial-style buildings. My guess was that the area was prone to flooding, thus the raised sidewalks, which were as high as the roof level of the many cars parked on the street.

The bus driver was forced to slow down a bit and navigate through the cars parked on both sides, but he didn't think twice about taking out several side mirrors on those vehicles. There was more grumbling from the peanut gallery, but no one voiced their concern, now in mortal fear of the crazy bus driver and his sidekick.

The narrow road had narrowed even more by the time the bus made it to the last parked car—which was on the bus driver's side. The bus became wedged between the high sidewalk to the right and the car to the left. Frustrated, he actually accelerated, and the bus literally picked up the parked car, carrying it scraping and crunching along between the bus and the raised sidewalk. The bus dragged the sedan, pinned between the sidewalk's high wall and the side of the bus, for about 20 feet, finally releasing the now-battered car once the street widened enough. Not one person on the bus uttered a word. I imagined they were now praying, hoping they would survive this horrible ordeal.

Once we were free of the downtown traffic, the bus pulled up to the museum. We were told that another bus would pick us up in two hours. It's customary to tip a driver and guide when disembarking, and it was interesting to see how many people paid more than usual—normally, most Americans are cheap when it comes to tipping drivers and guides, but today I saw many $5 and $10 bills being gladly handed over. I wasn't sure if it was because the trip was so exciting, or they feared the dynamic duo, or because they were happy to have made it there safely.

Wanting to be the last to leave, so I could take my time thanking Jorge and the driver, I motioned for the Ugly Americans to go ahead of me. When the lady made her way to the front, she couldn't help herself any longer. A verbal tirade ensued, with her doing most the talking. She told the driver and Jorge she was going to report them to the authorities and to the American Embassy and to the tour operator and this and that and blah, blah, blah. Jorge smiled and simply said, "This is how we do things in our country. Those cars are not to be parked on that street, and the signs clearly state this."

His answer didn't appease the woman, who was now in full rage. Jorge sweetly asked her if she would like a personal tour of the "prison, ah, museum," noting that the cells were still there and sometimes used, when needed. The woman shut up immediately and got off the bus as quickly as she could, along with the rest of her group. I laughed so hard I cried, and when I recovered, I gave both men a $20 tip and thanked them for the exciting excursion. And note: I never did see the Ugly Americans inside the museum.

When traveling abroad, it's best to relax, go with the flow and enjoy the locals and their ways. And what about writing that article on Belize for the U.S. papers? I never did, scared that Eldon would read it and then try to one-up my wonderful Belize bus driver. I hope he doesn't read this book or I'm in for the ride of my life.

Top: Museum of Belize

Bottom: Croc looking for something to eat.

The
Great Outdoors

Mother Nature is always full of surprises!

Uncle Roy vs. GPS

by

Patrick Sisti

As an outdoor travel writer mainly focusing on the Adirondack region of upstate New York, I've been really fortunate in my 60 years to have had my own personal outdoor guide.

There's a man named Leroy Spring who lives in Indian Lake, New York. He's also my "Uncle Roy" who has taught me everything—and I mean everything—I know about the great outdoors.

My lessons started at about age five and have continued throughout my life, the latest coming just last Sunday. My favorite thing to do in my life right now is hiking back into Adirondack ponds where I camp overnight and fish for brook trout. Well, I had recently taken a course on *How to Use a GPS* at the Adirondack Mountain Club in Lake George. With my new outdoor skill, I plotted out a hike to a relatively obscure pond. It took me about an hour, calculating, measuring, adding and subtracting latitude and longitude and entering the numbers into my GPS. When I was all finished and felt secure enough to believe my entries, I was ready to venture forth.

But first, I had to call Uncle Roy and tell him about my travel plans, in case something happened to me. I told him what pond I'd be going to, where my car would be parked, what route I'd be taking, how long I'd be gone, and when I would be back out. I gave him all my information and explained proudly that I was going to bushwhack about one-half mile using my GPS since my topo maps didn't show any marked trails. His reply floored me.

"Well," Uncle Roy said, "if you go to the top of the hill, there's an old apple tree there. Next to the apple tree, there used to be an old tote road. You can take that down the hill most of the way."

He didn't stop there.

"When it turns right and goes up a hill, you keep walking straight ahead down the hill. You'll come into some swampy area and tag alders. Keep walking straight ahead. About 400 feet beyond that is the pond," he said, then added, "Now, I haven't been there in many years, but look for that apple tree on top of the hill anyway. Call me when you get out."

I stood silent after we said our goodbyes and hung up. *Go to the top of the hill, there's an old apple tree there. Next to the apple tree, there used to be an old tote road. You can take that down the hill most of the way. He hasn't been there in man years?* I mumbled to myself. At age 87, "many years" could be 50 or 60 to Uncle Roy!

I looked at the GPS in my hand. I looked at the topo map

on my kitchen counter with all my markings on it. I looked at all my scraps of paper I used in my calculations. I looked at the five pencils and erasers I used. I looked at my 36-inch straight-edge ruler I had used to draw my lines on the topo map. Then I looked at the phone.

Why do I even bother? I should have called Uncle Roy first and told him where I was going and asked him how to get there. It would have saved me one hour of my life. It would have been like being in New York City and flagging down a cab—you get in and tell the taxi driver where you want to go and then sit back and enjoy the view. But in the Adirondacks, you call Uncle Roy. He'd tell me what tree to turn at. Where to go up or down a hill. To go through the hardwoods or the pines. Cross the brook. Stay out of the blow-down. Go around the swamp. Follow the little brook to the pond.

I stood there for a moment, and then smiled. My smile got bigger and bigger until I started laughing. That smile stayed with me all afternoon while I hiked in and out of the pond using my high-tech GPS and my topo map with all my plot lines. Oh, yes! The apple tree was at the top of the hill. And, yes, there was an old tote road next to the apple tree. And, yes, the road went down the hill. And, yes, it turned to the right and went uphill. And, yes, I continued straight down the hill into a swampy area where the tag alders were. And guess where the pond was? Yep, 400 feet straight ahead.

Who needs a GPS when you have Uncle Roy?

They Only Come Out at Night

by
Gregory Lamping

Years ago my wife, Mary, and I would travel around the countryside searching for places to camp. We would spot an area on the map and think, *Hmm, this might be an interesting place to stay for the night, let's give it a whirl!* We often had no idea what we were getting ourselves into.

"Hey, here's a place!" I said to Mary, looking at a Missouri map. "It's along a creek that flows into Truman Lake." I wanted to go fishing.

We stopped off at a general store in Osceola. I asked the owner about the area and he said, "You can camp there. The fishing is great. But remember, if it starts to rain, get the hell out. That area is known for its flash floods."

Once I heard the fishing was GREAT, we were on our way.

We camped at the end of a narrow dirt road, parking several yards from the creek. As soon as I opened the back door, our beagle, Buster, rushed out, sniffing the ground. He quickly caught a scent and started howling.

"We better keep him tied up," I told Mary.

After setting up the tent, I tripped over a guy line—an outside cable or rope used to help stabilize a tent—and accidentally kicked a hole in our home away from home. I yelled an obscenity, took a deep breath and looked over the damage. I thought, *Oh well, just as long as something doesn't try crawling through that hole at night.*

I fished while Mary sat watching me fish. After a while, she got bored and decided to drive into town to buy a magazine. When she tried to turn the car around, she lost sight of the road and backed into the swamp. She floored the accelerator and spun the rear tires until the car was hopelessly mired in the mud. We were stuck for the night, come hell or high water.

Once it got dark, we went to bed. A thick cover of clouds had moved in, so there were no stars or moonlight. Our only light was a flashlight.

I lay back on a foam mattress pad, listening to the night sounds: the crickets chirping, the bullfrogs croaking, the owls hooting and some godforsaken creature that sounded like a banshee screeching her fool head off. I had almost drifted off to sleep when I felt something crawling on my face. Reflexively, I slapped it just as it was crossing my lips. I instantly found out that a daddy longlegs, when squished, secretes this goop that tastes and smells like putrid goat cheese. I sputtered it out, sat up and grabbed the flashlight.

"Look—its legs are twitching!" I said to Mary, as I pointed the flashlight at its mangled body quivering on the tent floor.

"Kill it!" she said.

"I did!"

"Kill it again!"

I carefully picked it up by one of its legs, but it broke off. I was left holding this very long, very skinny leg that was still twitching. Buster had to sniff the spider before I swept it up with my hand and shook it outside.

We tried going to sleep, but we could sense this was going to be a "Now what?!" night. We soon heard something scratching at the paper bag outside our tent. We guessed at what it could be.

"It's a skunk," I told Mary.

"Are you sure?"

"Smell it."

"What are you going to do?"

"Let it have the Oreos." It had evidently just sprayed its load, but for all I knew, it could still have a backup plug of stink juice packed in its butt with our names on it.

"Do you think it'll come into the tent?"

"No, it can't." Then I remembered that hole. We lay still, afraid that any sudden noise might cause the skunk to fire off another round. I wanted it to eat so many of our cookies that it would waddle away with a big belly and smile on its face. It kept scratching at the bag for several minutes before finally giving up and moving on. I wasn't about to cry out, "Hey, Stinky! Guess what? Bags have OPENINGS!"

Later in the night, I was leaning back, hands behind my head, eyes closed, when—"YAAAAAA!!!"

"What's the matter?" Mary asked.

"Something just hit me in the back!"

It felt as if a ghoul were clawing his way up from the ground and had punched me in the back, angry that I had pitched our tent over his grave. Or maybe it was a mole.

Seconds later, it did it again and I yelled that same yell, but this time, I sat up and began pounding the floor of the tent with my fist, playing my own version of Whack-A-Mole. I wasn't sure if I had smacked my target, but it didn't happen again. I imagine the mole thought the Gods must be crazy.

I believed that if I tried really hard by giving it the old college try, I could fall asleep. Instead, we heard coyotes. They seemed far, far away at first, but their yapping kept getting closer and closer. Buster heard them as well, rose up from his slumber, and then launched into a howl that translated to, *Come on, ya punks . . . I'll take you on!*

"Buster, shut up!" I yelled. I was in no mood to fend off a pack of coyotes eager to find out who that stupid creature was inside our tent, begging for a fight. Mary grabbed Buster in her arms, trying to soothe his raging male ego.

Suddenly, we heard a loud splash. It was either a pot-bellied werewolf jumping into the creek for a late-night swim or a deer. My mind started to race, and my heart did its best to keep up. *It's a deer being chased by coyotes and swimming toward our camp and some hungry carnivores are going to be circling around our tent wondering if THERE'S ANYTHING TASTY TO EAT INSIDE HERE!!*

I was ready to protect my family. My plan was to get down on all fours and whenever one of them coyotes stuck its head through the hole in our tent, I was going to pop it in the nose! I figured we would survive, just as long as I kept punching them. But then we heard this ominous sound: pit . . . pat . . . pit . . . pat . . . then . . . PLAT! PLAT! PLAT!

The raindrops were big and coming down hard, amplified by the drumming on the tent. "It's raining," Mary said.

Yeah, I know.

"Didn't that guy at the store tell us that if it started to rain . . ."

Yeah, I know.

We became increasingly more anxious as it continued to rain and rain and rain. Because we could get swept away by a flash flood, we gave up on falling asleep. So we just lay back wondering how long it would have to rain before we would need to dash out of the tent, climb up a tree and hold on for our dear lives.

Then I realized something horrible—I had to pee. I would have to step out of the tent in my shorts and T-shirt and stand in the cold, hard rain. Otherwise, I would not be able to rid my body of those beers I drank earlier that evening. There was no otherwise. When ya gotta go, ya gotta go.

Though it was July, every raindrop that pelted my body felt like December. I wanted to be done quickly with what I had to do and get back in the tent, but the more I hurried, the more I struggled, in fits and starts.

Earlier in the day, I had seen this little gully alongside our tent. Illuminated by flashes of lightning, I looked up and noticed that it was now as wide as the creek. *The flood was coming!* Or so I thought. Actually, it was the creek I was looking at, but I was too disoriented by the rainstorm to think clearly. I crawled back into the tent and told Mary that we were doomed, that the floodwaters were rising incredibly fast.

"That does it!" she said. "First thing in the morning, we're getting the hell outta here!"

"Our car's in the mud."

"We'll run!"

In the morning, we awoke to sunlight. Songbirds were singing. Butterflies were flying. Grasshoppers were hopping. The leaves were gently blowing in the breeze. It was a beautiful world. The previous night seemed like nothing more than the shadow of a nightmare.

We heard tires rumbling down the road and saw a truck headed our way. A pleasant man with three-day-old whiskers stepped out. I saw he had a couple of fishing rods in the back of his pickup. I smiled.

"Is that yur car?" he asked.

"Yeah, that's ours," I said. "Can you help us? I got a rope."

"Shore!" he said, the most blessed word I had ever heard.

By noon, we had packed up and were back on the road, looking at a map.

"Hey, here's a place!"

A young coyote looking for lunch.

Patience in Princeton, BC

by
Lisa McManus Lange

At the request to go dock-fishing, I promptly put down my eyelash curler like the devoted mother I am and followed The Mighty Fisherman out the cabin door—with only one set of my lashes properly curled.

And when The Mighty Fisherman is a 10-year-old boy who has been waiting all year to fish at the family lakeside cabin, you best do as you're told and follow.

Only moments before I had washed my hair with water from a hose outside, treated lake water as cold and pure as the forest around us. The circling turkey vultures overhead were likely waiting for me to drop dead of brain freeze.

With my Jackie-O sunglasses firmly in place—dared not let a bear see my one set of non-curled eyelashes—I sat in the sun drying my hair while The Mighty Fisherman readied his tackle.

For 45 minutes.

I should say "I sat in the sun *patiently*."

I could have curled my other eyelashes during this time, but I didn't want to portray disinterest. Instead, I entertained myself by contemplating all the trend-setting, jewelry-making possibilities of the fishing tackle in The Mighty Fisherman's box.

So I continued to wait—*patiently*.

At 30 kilometers in the bush, time and patience are pretty much all you have—but with a few extras. The dock in question floated precariously on Missezula Lake, found just north of Princeton, British Columbia, with a subdivision of 80 or so cabins huddled around one end. With electricity and water luckily available, year-round residents in neighboring houses luxuriate in hot water baths, while I resort to cold-water mornings. But my complaining stops there, as plumbing in all capacities is available. As long as there were flush toilets, I considered myself the toughest female in the bush.

Every year we make the five-hour trek to the family summer cabin at the request of my in-laws, to reunite with other family we haven't seen since the previous summer. And like the 10-year-old's demands that are best followed, so are the requests of my in-laws.

Finally, The Mighty Fisherman announced he was ready, and off we went.

As The Mighty Fisherman and I trudged out to the end of the dock, he was sure-footed, whereas I was not. The movement of the dock, in sync with the waves from passing motorboats, didn't faze him. I, on the other hand, reassured myself with the excuse that my lack of sea legs was due to my unbalanced, unevenly curled eyelashes.

Without a word or backward glance to make sure his poor

mother hadn't fallen into the water, The Mighty Fisherman set about opening the container of worms and his tackle box (did I see a pair of school scissors in there?) and readied his rod.

I, on the other hand, finally made it close enough to him to assist if necessary, yet far away enough to prevent my ponytail from getting caught on a flying hook as he cast out. I figured sitting was safer than standing, but better yet, lying down was safer than sitting. I attempted to recline gracefully, waiting for the luxurious lull of the waves to relax me. With my Jackie-O sunglasses firmly in place, I *knew* I looked the part of a tough outdoorswoman.

But instead, I flopped like a fish from back to front, trying to get comfortable. Nothing worked. Not only were the fish laughing at me from below, but I was positive the scavengers circling above were, yet again, waiting for me to die—but this time, however, from an infection from slivers I was acquiring in places we will not discuss here. I gave up, sat up and grabbed a life vest from a nearby moored boat to use as a seat cushion, the fear of sliver-infection outranking my concern over the owners of the boat.

As The Mighty Fisherman muttered to himself while doing fisherman things I didn't understand, I focused on having happy, reflective thoughts. My mind wandered to all the writing fodder I could glean from this trip to the great outdoors. Why didn't I think to bring a paper and pen with me? At least I could have made paper airplanes to ward off the buzzing mosquitoes—they really had it out for me.

The Mighty Fisherman then reeled in, and more muttering ensued (I am pretty sure I heard "stupid fish" among his ramblings). He fiddled with the hook and cast off again.

And then for the longest time . . . we waited.

And waited.

And waited some more.

My thoughts bounced from my eyelashes to the slivers in unmentionable areas to writing.

As for him, his patience was remarkable for a 10-year-old. He reeled in and instead of giving up, he changed hooks, flies, bobbers or lures—whatever they were—and cast out again.

And patiently waited.

Again.

Just sitting there.

I asked his back, "What are you thinking about?"

"I'm figuring out what to use next," came his thoughtful reply.

At that moment, I was reminded of what life was all about.

Patience.

Like having patience during the five-hour drive to the lake, my husband keen on making "good time," while my legs are crossed waiting for the next pit stop. *Patience.* Like responding to my in-laws' requests. *Patience.* Like chatting and mingling with family I haven't seen since the previous year, when all I want to do is curl up on a lawn chair and enjoy my vacation. *Patience.* Like The Mighty Fisherman whose persistence keeps him returning to the dock, waiting for the one that got away, his only prize being sunburnt ears. *Patience. Remember, we're on vacation,* I told myself.

When finally we had waited long enough, I began to feel a prickling on my own ears. I realized my ears were likely burning from the blazing sun, the heat likely uncurling my one and only perfectly curled set of lashes. It was time to head in.

With reluctance he agreed, because frankly, he was "getting hungry anyways." *Thank God I don't have to gut a fish tonight*, was my only thought. The Mighty Fisherman's shoulders slouched in defeat. Skunked again.

As he packed up his tackle box, his school scissors positioned just so, I asked The Mighty Fisherman what he planned to use on our next trip.

His one word answer: "Wieners."

And whaddya know—they worked.

The Mighty Fishermen (Matthew, wearing cap) finally caught the big one with the help of his brother, Mitchell, and a little patience.

Beauty and the Beasts

by
Kathy Pippig

After pulling the truck and tent trailer into a double-wide spot in the small parking lot, we stepped out and walked to the edge of the escarpment.

There before us lay the grand vista of the valley. Crisp, cool air swirled around us as we crowded with others at the outlook, gazing at the breathtaking view. We stretched out our arms and pointed at a great waterfall in the distance, and then to the half-domed rock, capped in clouds and illumined in a column of sun from the south. We took in the massive protruding wall of granite to the left and the arches that ages ago had been created in the walls of the valley. Below, the valley floor was carpeted with verdant meadows and thick with trees.

We climbed back into our vehicle and drove on until we reached the Lower Pines Campground. After setting up camp, we had a bite of lunch and relaxed.

Off to the west, in a meadow of small, reedy pockets of swampy earth and dried yellow grasses, grazed a herd of mule deer, nearly obscured but for their long ears poking above their delicately shaped heads and slender necks. I walked closer to get a better look. Their heads followed my course from the camp to the meadow. We studied each other—the deer and I—and none of us moved. Cars sped by on the road past the meadow. Campers arrived, shuffling about in their designated camps. Hikers and bicyclists scurried back and forth on the paths around us. But the deer and I remained quiet, unmoving.

I glanced up at Half Dome and spotted dots of color and movement on its crest—hikers. I swiveled my gaze to the opposite side of the valley. I followed the upper ridge, and my eyes stopped. There, rushing down the slope of granite, Yosemite Falls pulsed torrents of snow-melted water over rocky ledges, down the cliff wall, and down farther still, crashing at the bottom in a spray of mist. Rainbow patterns winked in and out of the dewy spray.

When I got back to camp, several people were whispering to each other and gesturing toward something moving through the nearby trees. Everyone was looking at the same thing. I looked, too. Between shafts of sunlight, columns of shadow and the trees, a large coyote strolled past us and on to the river on the other side of the camp. We gasped with delight.

Later that night during supper, a park ranger visited each group of campers. She advised us that there was a large indigenous bear population in the park. She instructed us to store all foods in the iron bear-proof storage boxes. And not just food. Anything with an attractive scent was to go in these boxes—not in our vehicles, tents, campers or RVs—but in the iron storage box.

We did as she had instructed. Others did not.

That night, while the humans slept in their sleeping bags, beds or cots, bears came to visit—a mama and her two cubs. We didn't discover this until the next morning. My brother remarked that he had heard a soft shuffling sound outside his tent that night. He had peeked through the window of the tent and watched as the mother bear and her cubs ambled past his tent and on to the campground across the road. There, the bears totally destroyed the campers' van.

We discovered that she also had paid us a call. She had left her paw prints on our truck, and some on the outside wall of the tent trailer, just above the place where my head had rested that night in sleep.

Yosemite is a place of wonder. But I wonder about something more. When I think about the magnificent creatures who dwell there, and then about the hordes of humans who visit the valley, I often ask myself, *Which are the beasts?*

Yosemite
National Park
campground

Lounge or Lunge

by
Laurel McHargue

In an attempt to acquaint our sons with the many wonders of Colorado, Mike and I would plan adventures to take us away from the comforts of our Colorado Springs home. One adventure brought us to Leadville, where Mike competed in his first pack burro race, putting us on a mailing list for the Western Pack Burro Ass-ociation. It's a real thing, and the name is indeed hyphenated. So when we received an invitation to the organization's annual banquet, and we hadn't yet discovered the town of Salida, we packed our bags for a new adventure, taking sons Nick, age 14 and Jake, age 12, with us.

Upon arrival, we realized that we had four options for what to do the following day. The Weather Channel was reporting a possible approaching snowstorm coming over the mountains, so we were prepared to have our choices limited by the time we woke up. Our options:

1. Attend the donkey training seminar at the fairgrounds (what the Ass-ociation would want);
2. Shop in the quaint, historic town of Salida;
3. Lounge luxuriously in the soothing hot springs just across the street; or
4. Climb the local Mount Shavano, all 14'er feet of it. It's called a "14'er" because its peak is more than 14,000 feet high.

I really thought we should attend the bonding-with-your-burro event. After all, we had just won a burro brush at the banquet that night. As the boys pointed out, "Now all you need is the accessory." Not yet the proud owners of Bobby—what we'll surely name our first burro whenever we get him—Mike was disinclined just to watch as others who dragged their own asses to the weekend festivities learned how to maneuver donkey obstacle courses, or whatever the training actually included. No, we would not attend the donkey training. Not this year.

Shopping. *Brrrr.* I still get shivers when I recall the countless hours of digging through bins at The Bargain Center in Quincy, Massachusetts, as a child. No dressing rooms—no real order to what you might be looking for—but boy, could Mom find a bargain. Hours and hours of power shopping, of back-aching standing around as Mom would feel every item on every hanger, or of us hiding in the racks of clothes to avoid having to try on one more winter coat that was on sale because it was still 98 degrees outside. No, we would not go shopping.

To be fair, I already knew that the first two choices weren't real options. So when Mike said that we may not be able to climb Mount Shavano because of the storm coming in that night, I tried very hard to mask my excitement over the possibility of choice #3. Gee. Would we possibly not have to wake up extra early to get a head start on attacking the mountain before it got really bad? Would we possibly have to spend a leisurely morning—after a nice home-style breakfast at the local diner—soaking, floating, easing our burdens away in the natural hot springs across the street from our hotel? Golly, I hoped not.

After a fitful night's attempt at sleep, we awoke later than expected to a beautiful morning. Damn. There were clouds in the sky, but they weren't even ominous. We were allowed a few minutes to grab a cold, hard pastry in the motel lobby before heading out on our quest to "bag another 14'er." This was Mike's and Nick's quest; Jake and I were happy to shoot for a 13.5'ish-er.

OK, I'll admit it: the day was spectacular, and we ended up with an unexpected surprise—two seasons in one day. The aspens were at their peak intensity for autumn color, and when it started to snow, the whole scene became a fairyland.

The trail up Mount Shavano was well worn, and husband Mike and eldest son Nick quickly disappeared as they advanced on their speed ascent. We had walkie-talkies, so I felt confident that Jake and I would enjoy the adventure at our own pace. But I should admit something here. Long ago and far away, I would let other fellow mountain hikers know that I would "hang back" with Jake. Yes, I would sacrifice the painful thin-air-sucking experience so that Jake could build his confidence. Yes, I might not even make it to the top. I would do that. But something changed the year when Jake turned 12. Something both beautiful and tragic.

I had to ask Jake to slow down (OK, to STOP) a couple times.

This was beautiful because it demonstrated that my little boy was now both full of confidence and ability. It was tragic because, well, I couldn't keep up with him anymore.

He was very patient with me, though, and as we had done on countless past adventures, while Nick and his Dad were focused on the *top*—and I'm not suggesting there's anything wrong with that—Jake and I embraced the *around*. We took in the expanse of emerald green-covered boulder fields along several hillsides. We were amazed by what looked like a foot-high flame carved into the bottom of a burnt-out tree trunk. We bounced on old pines bent low across our path yet still rooted in the earth. We scooped up and ate handfuls of the season's first snow. We laughed at the gray face of stone at our feet with a protrusion of fleshy pink rock that looked just like a tongue sticking out at us.

The air was fall-winter fresh, and our steady journey up the mountain yielded peeks of peaks as the sun would occasionally break through the clouds and falling snow. Three hours into the adventure, we got to a point, after having ascended from a long saddle in the mountain, where we thought we could see the end of our journey. But there were three distinct summits, and when we called Nick, who beat his Dad to the top this time, we learned that they had reached the peak and were heading down. Protected as we were in the saddle, we hadn't experienced the blowing snow and wind they were feeling up top.

And so, having hiked to about 13.5'ish feet, Jake and I were happy to begin our descent, knowing that, at some point, Mike and Nick would catch us. Almost to the bottom, I sensed that we may have taken a wrong turn somewhere back up the hill. I didn't remember what lay before me, and I couldn't find any footprints.

Although the path ascending the mountain was obvious, things don't always look the same in reverse. But Jake was certain that we were on the right path, and not wanting to wait in place while I continued my search for footprints, he suggested that we just keep going. After all, we were still going downhill.

Jake was right, of course. We were on the correct path, and within minutes, we could hear the voices of our speed racers. We all enjoyed together what was left of the descent and were able to appreciate the grandeur of the aspen field that awaited us at the bottom. The trees were so large I could barely wrap my arms completely around them (yes, I hugged a tree), and the leaves were a glorious golden yellow.

I have come to realize that though my inclination is often to choose the least stressful of available options on any given day, I am inevitably delighted with what results from a decision to push beyond my comfort level. Yes, the hot springs would have been blissful, but our adventure on the mountain was heavenly.

Laurel hugging an aspen tree.

The Big One

by
Cliff Johnson

During the summer of 1988, my wife, Scharre, our two teenage daughters and I took a family camping trip along the West Coast, working our way north from California to Oregon and then into the San Juan Islands of Washington.

Four days into the trip, we stopped at a campground on the Oregon coast. After we set up camp, the girls and I went to check out the fishing at the mouth of a nearby river that dumped into the ocean. Scharre stayed behind—she disliked the sport because the damn fish always took her bait, interrupting her from reading her romance novels.

We found a boat dock and decided to try our luck from the comfort of our lawn chairs. The dock was nearly 50 feet long. The girls set up at one end of the dock and I at the other, which was a wonderful arrangement since it wouldn't cramp their style should any boys wander by. I left the net and some bait with them and returned to my spot for an afternoon of relaxed fishing.

A few people were fishing between the girls and me, and other campers also walked by to check out the action. After an hour of no activity, my pole started to stutter from small nibbles. Then, to my amazement, the pole almost bent in half. My immediate impression was that I had hooked either a whale or an aircraft carrier. I yelled to the girls, "Get the net. I've got a big one!"

Activity on and around the dock stopped as everyone anxiously watched the big one being landed. As my line started to clear the surface, it became slack—I feared my trophy had gotten away. By this time, my two daughters were standing by with the net. As I reeled in my line, it brought to the surface the smallest fish ever hooked outside of a goldfish bowl. It would be an exaggeration to say it was three inches long. When the girls saw the size of my fish, they began laughing so hard they nearly fell into the river. Even the crowd that had gathered to watch the great fisherman joined in the laughter.

Embarrassed, I stared down into the river when, suddenly, a seal stuck its head out of the water, and I swear it was wearing a mischievous smile on its face. I told the girls that the seal must have had a hold of the fish until it got near the surface, causing my pole to bend as it did. They said, "Oh sure, Dad," and laughed even more.

That evening, we were sitting around the campfire fighting off mosquitoes when my youngest daughter, Shayla, pointed at one and yelled, "Get the net!" Periodically, during the remainder of our trip, this phrase became a favorite of my wife and daughters, who would yell it, good-naturedly, with very little provocation every chance they got.

By the end of our family vacation, I had learned a very important lesson: It's best that the big one gets away . . . and nobody knows about it.

Oregon coast

Creature Feature

by
Ernie Witham

Sometimes I get to see something so amazing that I just have to share it with others. This sighting happened when my wife and I were at John Pennekamp Coral Reef State Park in the Florida Keys during a recent vacation.

It was 11 A.M. We had been to the visitor center and learned all about Florida's coral reefs, which took 5,000 to 7,000 years to develop—bet a lot of restaurants went out of business waiting for that tourist attraction to come to fruition. We were scheduled to go out on the noontime snorkeling boat for a close-up look at the reef and an hour-and-a-half of swimming with the fishes, but that wasn't quite enough for my wife.

"Let's check out Canon Beach," she said, pointing at the little cove just beyond the visitor center. "I want to try out the snorkeling equipment."

"You want to get all wet before the boat ride? You could catch a cold or something."

"It's 90 degrees," she said. "Come on."

"What about all our stuff? Someone has to keep an eye on things."

"Wimp," she said, playfully.

"Excuse me? I'm being the responsible one here for once."

"Er-nie's a wimmmpp. Er-nie's a wimmmpp."

I was still formulating a comeback when she went down to the water's edge and slipped on her flippers and mask. I thought about chasing after her, but something told me to wait. So I sat back and watched as she headed straight into the 85-degree water and just kept going until she was neck deep and a little farther out, I might add, than any of the other swimmers.

Ready for that amazing thing?

Just as she ducked under, this huge—I mean humongously huge—gray thing surfaced right in front of her. It looked like a cross between a submarine with a tail fin and an elephant without a trunk.

That's when she pulled her head out of the water, stood straight up and began walking backward as fast as her flippered feet would allow, which was incredibly fast. I can't ever remember seeing anyone in flippers move that fast before or since. In fact, she was striding backward at such a pace that she was creating a small wake and several kids had to scramble out of the way or get run over.

But she didn't stop at waist-deep. She didn't stop at thigh-deep, knee-deep or even ankle-deep. She just kept on striding backward right out of the water, onto the beach, and through the sand until she got to the picnic table under the shady palm tree where I was dutifully guarding our stuff.

"Did you see that?" I asked.

She gasped something I didn't quite understand.

"Yeah, I thought you must have. It was pretty big, huh?"

"Our house is big," she sputtered. "That thing was from a Japanese horror film. I expected to see Godzilla surface next to it and begin a battle to the death."

"According to this," I held up our guidebook, "the 'thing' you just had a close encounter with was a manatee. Says here they're docile and have doleful eyes."

"It touched me," she said.

"Probably just lonely. Some people find them endearing. Maybe you should have petted it, let it know you were a friend of the sea."

She looked at me like I was nuts.

"By the way, the Guinness people called to say you've set some kind of water-to-land speed record."

Now her look turned to one that was slightly deranged. So, as hard as it was, I withheld further comment.

A few hours later, as we were about to jump into the Atlantic Ocean and observe schools of parrot, angel and butterfly fish, the captain reminded us that there was a 9-foot-high "Christ of the Deep" bronze statue submerged several hundred yards away from the coral reef that we could swim to if we so wanted. It's supposed to be quite amazing, attracting divers from all over the world.

"Whataya think?" I asked. "Maybe we'll see your manatee friend."

"No freaking way," she said.

I smiled. "Pa-aatt's a wimmmpp. Pa-aatt's a wimmmpp."

It took several days for the mark on my butt—made by my wife's right flipper—to go away. But believe me, it was worth it.

Hither
and Yon

Here, there and everywhere!

Glamour on the Go

by
Dena Harris

Fueled by a lifetime of reading *Vogue* and *O* magazines, here's my dream packing scenario for international travel. I'd include kicky, sophisticated outfits that transition effortlessly from day to night with the simple addition of a silk scarf, heels and hoop earrings. I'd add unwrinkled, perfumed silky undergarments for day, accompanied by naughty lingerie for passionate nighttime romps in luxurious hotel rooms. Topping off this dream are strappy stilettos that cushion my feet as I bounce around the cobblestoned streets of Amsterdam and Italy.

As a seasoned international traveler, let me share with you the reality of what I actually pack into my suitcase. I select long-sleeved cotton and linen clothing that is neither kicky nor sophisticated, but does prevent hospitalization for sun rash treatment while traveling in hot Muslim countries. I've learned that the bland beige and white Ex-Officio travel underwear called "wicking"—because the weave prevents moisture from collecting on the skin—can be washed out nightly in the hotel room sink, making it possible to travel for months with only two pairs of underwear. And take it from me, nothing says romance like his and her wicking underwear drying side-by-side on the towel rack. "Breathable" bras and full-cut panties are a must, because just one time wandering around Paris with a full-on wedgie from sexy thong underwear is one time too many. And rounding out the bottom of my travel suitcase are always five beautiful filmy scarves I convince myself I will use to update and transition my outfits from day to night. But the scarves never actually see the light of day because the reality is I live 90 percent of my life in sweatpants and have no idea how to use an accessory to update an outfit.

Instead of fashionable heels, I'm toting gym shoes and Birkenstocks around the globe. And yes, I will wear both with evening dresses because I'm long past my 20s and the universal truth that comfort trumps style has been revealed to me.

Sadly—and more than a little unfairly—women in the glamour magazines and movies don't have to deal with the reality of airline travel. I don't think the 19-year-old model on the cover of this month's issue of *More* magazine has been cavity searched like the rest of us for attempting to smuggle on a jar of facial crème so our poor dehydrated skin has a chance to look decent upon arrival at our destination. Hear me now, fellow travelers: I will hand over the firming lotion, but when airport security tries to take my advanced formula crème that staves off under-eye wrinkles, I will single-handedly take down the entire TSA infrastructure. We all have our limits.

And don't get me started on packing food. For some reason I always target a trip abroad as the perfect time to lose those last five pounds. The reasoning goes that since I'll be trapped in a flying steel coffin for 18 hours, why not fast? Except I've never been one to get on a plane without food. While other travelers pack Sudoku and the latest *New York Times* bestseller, my carry-on is stuffed with a lifetime's worth of nuts, raisins, granola bars, oatmeal and peanut-butter crackers. Theoretically, I bring all this food so I'll have snacks for the duration of my trip, in case there's ever a day I'm stuck for a meal. But the reality is that I eat most of the food I pack before the first plane ever leaves the boarding gate.

So, I find glamour in wicking underwear, ugly shoes, dry skin and Lance's peanut-butter cracker breath . . . and I wouldn't choose to see the world any other way.

Dena

How to Err in Italian

by
David Carkeet

DAY 1: We arrive at the hotel in Rome mid-afternoon. I can't sleep. I leave my wife in the room and wander the streets. Young Romans stop me and ask in English what time it is. It's as if they can see the jet lag on my face and know I'm confused about the time. I've read that Italians are fond of subtle mockery. Here it is already.

DAY 2: My guidebook says that *prego* means "you're welcome." This is a lie. Prego means "you're doing something wrong again." From a museum guard it means you've entered without a ticket, or you're going the wrong way, or you can't use those stairs. From a subway official, it means that the token you're trying to give him, purchased from a machine deceptively near his station, is for the public telephone, not the subway.

To travel is to err. To err in Rome is to get a prego.

DAY 3: They keep asking me in English what time it is.

They do it only when they're part of a group, so I have a new theory: they're showing off their English to their friends. But I still feel mistreated. I'm a windup toy. Hey, look, an American! Let's make him speak English!

At lunch the Italian couple seated at the next table is talking about us, I can tell. When I respond to something my wife says with a "Yeah," the guy hears it as a *ja,* puts the ja together with my blond hair, and says knowingly to his companion, "Deutsch." A nation of showoffs. Quickly, loudly, I say, "Yes!" to my wife. Guess again, pal.

DAY 4: Mealtime is a bookish enterprise. My reference guide is *Harrap's Super-Mini Italian and English Dictionary* ("Acclaimed as the Finest of Its Kind on the Continent"). I look up *melanzana* and it says *aubergine*. What in the hell is an aubergine? I realize Harrap has puzzled me like this before. Suspicious, I check the copyright page. Harrap is for Brits! The waitress approaches and says, "Prego." In a restaurant, prego means "I'm ready to take your order even though you're not ready to give it to me." I give up on melanzana and point interrogatively at another listing on the menu. The waitress says this item has *pancetta* in it. She watches me flee to Harrap, which tells me pancetta means "pot-belly." I laugh and point to my belly and make a rounding gesture with both hands. The waitress stares. My wife, reading from her menu, says, "What's *cervello?*" The waitress interprets her question as an order and writes it down. I know that cervello means brains, and I wave my hands and cry, "No, no, no!" The waitress frowns at me. With a pang of despair, I feel that all of my interactions in life have been exactly like this one.

DAY 5: At the hotel breakfast buffet, the milk is sour. I must tell the waiter. Harrap gives me three words for "sour": *acido, acerbo* and *aspro*. I don't want to report the milk's pH, so I reject acido. Acerbo scares me. I can imagine the waiter telling the guys in the kitchen, "The American finds the milk acerbic." In mounting confusion, I likewise reject aspro. Let the other guests gag on the milk.

DAY 6: When I ask for directions, they answer as if I were fluent in Italian. They go on and on. I hear a *sinistra* here, a *destra* there; *avanti* waves hopefully to me from the distance. I can't put the main words together because of all the other words—function words, grace notes. I don't want elegance. I want caveman talk. Having asked for help, I have the urge to tell them to shut up.

DAY 7: My wife simply cannot remember that cervello means "brains." She asks me about it at every meal. I am able to remember it because I rely on cognates. I urge her to do the same. "Think of 'cervix,'" I say. "How's that going to help?" she asks. I say, testily, "The cervix is part of the brain." As she stares at me, I suddenly realize I've confused "cervix" with "cerebellum."

DAY 8: It is mid-afternoon and I am fading. I want a cup of coffee. I asked for coffee on an earlier occasion and was disappointed at the goods delivered—a tiny cup containing a few drops of essence of coffee. I suspected mockery and looked around for natives stifling laughter. When I asked the waiter how to get a big cup of coffee, he said I should ask for *caffè americano* or *caffè nero*.

Now, in this restaurant, I reject caffè americano because I don't want to proclaim that I have flown thousands of miles in order to drink American coffee, even though I have. I ask confidently for caffè nero. The woman shakes her head. "Tè nero," she says—black tea. I will not translate this successfully until the end of the day. At the moment, when it counts, when I am fading and could really use some black tea, I become locked in a rigid, inescapable misinterpretation. Because the Italian "t" can sound like a "d," I hear her two words as one: *dinero.* I think she is telling me that I can't buy coffee because coffee does not cost enough dinero. I arrive at this improbable conclusion because of two prior experiences.

First, the day before, when I tried to buy an *acqua minerale* in a restaurant, I got a shake of the head and a clear explanation, in different words, that I would need to buy a whole meal, which interested me even less than the acqua minerale—a pretext in the first place because I really just wanted to use the toilet. Second, I know that the dinar is the monetary unit of nearby Yugoslavia because earlier I got a five-dinar coin as change in a shop, throwing me into deep confusion. I conclude that dinar—or some variant of it—is a common regional term for money. Thus much learning, experience and reasoning synthesize to yield my ingenious interpretation of tè nero as dinero.

DAY 9 (morning): I have developed rules for walking in Rome. (1) Place your thumbnail on the map and inch it along as you walk, checking your progress every few steps; neglect this for a moment and you will become lost forever. (2) When crossing a street, look left, then right, then left again. It's astonishing how quickly a menace to your life can fill that empty space to the left.

These are good rules, but I cannot penetrate Italian sidewalk manners. The natives don't yield. They aim right for me and make me yield. I try to telegraph my intent ("I'll take the curb, signore, while you hug the building"), but it has no effect. I become aware of walking body language when a fellow American approaches and we start to exchange signals from a great distance. The messages are really flowing; we're sending volumes of information to each other. We pass without incident. This gets me thinking, *Maybe the natives give signals, but later than Americans, closer to the moment of passing.* I will look for the signs.

DAY 9 (evening): As a pedestrian, I am transformed. I wait for a late signal from the Italians, and I get it, though I wouldn't be able to say what form it takes. I just get it. I am bodily fluent. I glide through Rome. When I see approaching Americans start to fidget from a block away, I want to shout, "Don't be so uptight!"

DAY 10: I have found my caveman. He got us to a distant catacomb in fine style. Good with the hands and quick with the amplifying paraphrase. When he told us to turn at the *semaforo*, he didn't just leave it at that. With his hands he created three imaginary circles in the air, one above the other, and he said, "Semaforo. Rosso, ambra, verde. Semaforo." Donald Sutherland needed this guy in *Don't Look Now.*

DAY 11: If I had the Italian with me who thought I was a German, I would give him a new rule for identifying Germans. They look exactly like Americans except for their feet, which always are shod in funny footwear. As for Americans, you will know them by their laughter. It is loud. In groups it sounds strained, as if it masks deep pain. I've cut way down on my own laughter. Either you're going to glide or you're going to guffaw. You can't do both. Me, I'll glide.

DAY 12: It is our last day, and we rent a car for an excursion to outlying sites. But first, we must escape the city. I immediately develop three rules for driving in Rome:

1. If you have an advantage, keep it.
2. Don't send false messages.
3. If lost, follow someone.

An hour into the countryside, an iconic warning light appears in the dash—a line angling from the upper left to the lower right and intersecting a circle. The tiny image looks like a banking airplane on a collision course with us, but I don't think the car is equipped with radar. My wife wants me to stop and have the engine checked. I put it off for as long as possible, risking a roadside breakdown against guaranteed linguistic chaos in the service bay. But finally I relent and pull into a rural gas station. I beckon to the attendant, who is so strikingly good-looking that I wonder if I have driven onto a movie set. He leans down to my window. I point to the dash light and throw my hands up helplessly. He nods with excitement—he knows what it means.

But how to tell me? He doesn't have a morsel of English. He starts to speak and stops. He frowns. He starts and stops again. From out of nowhere I remember the signs posted near work sites at the Roman Forum, warning of danger. "Pericolo?" I ask. He brightens and says, "No pericolo. No pericolo." Then he sees a little lever in the dash above my knee and pulls it out. The engine revs. When he pushes it all the way in, the engine slows and the warning light disappears. The dash light is a signal for the manual fast idle, which my knee must have engaged. I go *vum, vum, vum* in imitation of the engine revving, and he grins and nods. I throw him a passionate grazie and speed away.

Driving down the road, I replay the moment of breakthrough. "Pericolo?" "No pericolo. No pericolo."

DAY 13: At the airport, all checked in and cleared, with Harrap in the hotel trash can and nothing on my mind, I watch two airport workers discuss something complicated about the ceiling near the gate. They have been discussing it for half an hour, even though the ceiling looks perfectly normal to me. They gesture, look overhead, look off in the distance, and look at each other. I watch one of them walk a few steps away and then come back—a bit of conversational behavior I have seen many times on this trip.

Here, now, I won't have to speak. I have nothing to say, nothing to ask. I should feel relieved, but I'm not. I realize I have developed a fondness for the halting transaction—the linguistic event in which a native meets you with what he's got, you meet him with what you've got, and your bodies work like the devil to make up for what neither of you has got. The natives, after all, want the same thing you want—to understand, to be understood.

The night before, in the hotel room, my wife asked me what I had liked best in Rome. The Colosseum? The Pantheon? The Baths of Caracalla? If she asked me now, I would point to my two Italians endlessly discussing the mystery of the ceiling.

"I like them best," I would say.

A Family Affair

by
Janis Dale

For the Dale family, being on the road is a family affair. My husband, daughters and I have journeyed the globe several times over and have no plans on stopping anytime soon. We are up for any adventure tossed our way and constantly live out of a suitcase or backpack. Having traveled to more than 80 countries, we have literally given our daughters the world, and they have learned much, as have we.

When we first met, my husband infected me with the travel bug after exploring Baja and mainland Mexico together. From there, we traveled far and near. To this day, I still refute my husband's claim that our first daughter was conceived among the trees in the Black Forest of Germany. After driving throughout Europe in a Volkswagen Beetle we purchased in Wolfsburg, we shipped the car to New York. Once back in the States, I was sick for the entire 3,000-mile trip from New York to California. I gave birth about nine months later to Dara.

Our family grew to three daughters—Dara, Erin and Ryan—and all three instantly took to the road with us. Travel is in their blood, and they have made fast friends all over the world. We have had grand adventures, including in country #42—Egypt. A memorable camel ride to the Pyramids was great until I had to pay *baksheesh*, a bribe, to the guide to stop him from making the camel RUN to the tombs. When I asked him later about the slaves who were led out of Egypt by Moses, he answered, "Moses who? There are many men named Moses." Interesting perspective!

Viewing animals in their natural habitats is a family favorite. Mind you, in Kenya, I wasn't overly excited about riding in an open-topped Land Rover in the savannah, looking for the Big Five wild beasts, until we did it. We were amazed. We saw giraffes eating from treetops, lions resting with babies under the trees and a beautiful leopard lounging on a tree limb. There were hundreds of animals large and small, birds that could run, not fly, and insects strange and deadly. And we did find the Big Five: rhino, lion, leopard, water buffalo and hippo. Plus wart hogs, elephants and wildebeest. And we even found human tribes—we stayed with the Masai people in a tent camp and sang Bob Marley songs around the campfire. It was amazing. We have since gone on at least a dozen safaris in African countries, and just as many animal treks in the Galapagos Islands and Central and South America.

We have witnessed our daughters literally walk on water in Baja California—escaping stingrays. We have seen a herd of elephants swim across Lake Karabi in Zimbabwe, just after recovering from watching our youngest daughter Ryan plunge off the bridge over the Zambezi River on a bungee cord. We have ridden the observation car on the train to the Copper Canyon in the state of Chihuahua in Mexico, where the canyon system is bigger and deeper than the Grand Canyon—right after the cow shit was cleaned off the car's floor, a little something courtesy of the prior bovine occupants. And in Costa Rica, riding the country's tallest and longest zip line through the forest canopy was a rush. Here we came face to face with howler monkeys and toucans. And one of the most memorable Costa Rican adventures was when our group got to see baby turtles hatch and run to the sea. Even our guide, Jorge, had tears in his eyes watching this once-in-a-lifetime event.

In Nepal, we have ridden elephants through the jungle looking for tigers. We saw paw prints, but no big cats, just your usual rhino hiding in the tall grass and a snake or two. In Mexico City, we paid a $120 bribe for instructions on how to get out of the city after driving in circles for five hours. And the cute little puppies we saw in a village in Thailand were going to be lunch or dinner for the families. From then on, we always questioned the mystery meat served on buffet tables.

In Borneo, Malaysia, we went on the hunt for headhunters. We found them—they were our guides! They told us they only took heads from other tribes as trophies when they battled over land. I think they secretly laughed at us when they showed us their shriveled collections. In the ultra-modern capital of Malaysia—Kuala Lumpar—I found the ultimate keep-the-husband-occupied-while-I-shopped technique; he sat with his feet in a pool of water. Seriously. But this pool was filled with little fish that nibbled on his toes, eating away all the dry skin on his feet. That day was an enjoyable experience for both of us.

In Nairobi, we visited the Carnivore Restaurant where Erin and Ryan declared themselves vegetarians after watching me eat crocodile, zebra and other wild treats. I did pass on the fried insects and tarantulas in Vietnam. We mustn't forget when our daughters—now much older—visited Ben Yehuda Street in Israel with a preacher's son. We found them in the hotel lobby the next morning, hung over! And it was in Mali, West Africa, where our youngest daughter took a serious liking to our tour guide and vice versa. Her dad and I are so glad she did not choose to move to Algeria with him.

Our daughters are now grown and married, so our new traveling companions have been our 10 grandchildren. When each grows old enough to travel alone with Grandma and Grandpa, we treat them to a big adventure. When granddaughter Carly turned 12, the three of us traveled to Dubai, where we went dune bashing in 4x4s and took a cruise on the Persian Gulf through the Strait of Hormuz, right at the time when Iran was challenging nearby countries with talk of nuclear attacks. But all went well, and we had a great trip, and Carly got a firsthand look at, understanding of and appreciation for other cultures, just as her mother and aunts did when we traveled with them.

Maya, our 10-year-old granddaughter, loved the Russian River Cruise from St. Petersburg to Moscow. She became the star of the ship in the Russian costume she wore for dinners. The latest trip was to the Bahamas and then to Disney World with four young grandkids. I am still recuperating!

Life on the road for the Dale family has been rewarding,

exhausting, exhilarating and amazing. The experiences we have shared as a family—and now with our extended family of sons-in-law, in-laws, grandchildren and close friends—is our way of life. We don't intend to stop anytime soon.

But we do have to hurry—we are getting much older, and the world, much smaller.

Top: The Dale family in Egypt.

Bottom: Erin with Masai in Kenya

Old Delhi, New Tricks

by
Farah Ghuznavi

The midday sun blazed overhead as Katy and I forged ahead, determined to do as much as possible before the melting caramel haze of the afternoon heat seeped into our bones and sapped our wills. We had yet to fully acclimatize, despite gladly swapping the autumn chill of London for the warmth of a week in India.

The morning had been well spent exploring Old Delhi, particularly the area around the Red Fort. The architecture dated back to the Mughal period of Muslim rule in northern India, and the building style was a wonderful mélange of arched entranceways and spacious apartments reaching up to touch soaring domed ceilings. Manicured gardens full of colorful blossoms and verdant plant life were everywhere, complemented by the luminous blades of emerald grass that sprang forth from every inch of ground.

As usual, we encountered a group of young men eager to try out their English. Fed up of negotiating this particular gauntlet, an inspired Katy decided to deny her British nationality and ethnicity in the hope of avoiding the stilted conversation that would most likely follow. In response to the inevitable, "Where are you from, sister?" query, she replied without batting an eyelid. "Norway."

The conversation that followed didn't quite go according to script. In amazement, a couple of the boys cried out, "Nowhere?! How can you be from nowhere?"

I stepped in to clarify, saying "She doesn't speak much English. She is from Norway. Do you know that place, N-O-R-W-A-Y?"

"Oh, yes, we know Norway," one of the boys answered gamely. He proceeded to respond in kind, "And we are from India, I-N-D-I-A!"

They were good sports and didn't pester us further, so we cooperated by posing for one of the group photos so close to the South Asian heart before moving swiftly on.

Born in neighboring Bangladesh, I had spent several intervening years studying and working in Britain. As a result, I was experiencing the peculiar disorientation of a brown foreigner on this trip. My Hindi was worse than rusty—more like fossilized, based as it was on a childhood diet of occasional Bollywood movies and a few family holidays.

An Indian friend in London had warned Katy that she shouldn't rely on my non-existent communication skills. "I don't know what language Farah's speaking, but it's certainly not Hindi!" she'd laughed, dismissing my halting attempts to articulate a few basic sentences. Luckily, my dubious language skills had been rendered largely redundant so far, given Indian enthusiasm toward practicing English.

Dipping into some of the souvenir shops near the entrance of the Red Fort, we emerged with treasures: sets of small glass animals in swirling shades of color, embroidered cloth wallets, hand-carved wooden miniature chess sets and white marble boxes inlaid with jewel-colored patterns of flowers and geometric shapes styled after the Taj Mahal marble work. Then there were Katy's favorites—small, red seeds hollowed out and filled with fragments of bone that were miraculously carved into tiny animal shapes and clearly visible through a magnifying glass.

After a reviving siesta at our hotel, we reemerged to venture into the crowded alleyways of Delhi West in search of the famous restaurant, Karim's. What followed was an orgy of grilled meats, kebabs on skewers and, so Katy could prove her adventure traveler credentials, a surprisingly delicious dish of sheep's brain *masala* accompanied by a selection of *rotis*—breads of various types and textures. A minor detour for the mandatory *paan* followed; a betel leaf and betel nut confection, garnished with a white paste notorious for providing a narcotic kick to the senses. Highly addictive, its side effects include a tendency to produce copious quantities of scarlet spit—though neither of us managed to keep it in our mouths long enough to experience the latter, this being most definitely an acquired taste.

Deciding to work off some of the gluttonous calories we'd absorbed, we headed for the nearby shrine of Nizamuddin, the mausoleum of the Sufi saint Nizamuddin Auliya. The Sufis belong to a Muslim sect that takes a distinctly peace-and-love approach to other religions and to humanity as a whole, emphasizing spirituality and coexistence. The place attracted people of all faiths and exuded a wonderful atmosphere of calm despite the crowds that had made their way there to worship. It was also featured in the controversial film *Fire* as the place where the lesbian protagonists found refuge after escaping domestic violence. We passed a couple of peaceful hours just people-watching and drinking in the atmosphere before making our way back to the main road.

I would like to blame what happened next on the narcotic in the paan, but that wouldn't be fair. Both of us had spat out the mangled green concoction into the nearest rubbish bin, me letting down my origins by doing so with unbecoming speed, even faster than Katy. But the sinful indulgence of that meat-heavy meal at Karim's may have had something to do with lulling us into a stupor of sorts. Or maybe we were just blissed out by our time at the shrine. Anyway, we climbed into one of the three-wheeled motorized scooters that litter the streets of Delhi and instructed the driver to take us back to our hotel in Jorbagh.

It was only after we'd been riding for some time that I began to get nervous about where we were heading. It seemed to be taking a lot longer on the way back than it had on the ride out. A few times, I reminded the driver that we wanted to go to Jorbagh. He nodded his head rhythmically back and forth in that uniquely Indian way that was presumably meant to be reassuring. But when we bypassed the city center and began heading into what looked like its outskirts, I could no longer dismiss my increasing sense of anxiety.

We didn't have to wait much longer for enlightenment of a distinctly non-Sufi nature. Drawing the scooter to a screeching halt on the side of a dusty road in decidedly unfamiliar surroundings, the driver indicated that we had arrived. The question was: Where were we? The place appeared to be some kind of industrial suburb, with no sign of any tourist accommodation in sight. Upon inquiry, the driver informed us that we were now in Karolbagh (which he pronounced to rhyme with our original destination, Jorbagh, as Krorebagh). If we now wanted to go to Jorbagh, which we should have told him in the first place, he asserted, it would cost us an extra 100 rupees!

I was outraged. It was the most obvious form of extortion. Clearly he had taken us both for idiotic foreigners who had no idea what they were doing. And the fact that he was partially right didn't make it any easier to swallow. Passersby began to stare at us with somewhat aggressive curiosity, since it was perfectly clear that we didn't belong there. With twilight fading into rapidly-descending night, and no other scooters or taxis to be seen, I didn't give much for our chances of finding our way home alone.

Katy stood by the roadside, looking more pale and more foreign by the minute, urging me to pay the man whatever he wanted to take us back to Jorbagh. But I'd had enough of being the brown alien. I couldn't help wondering if he would have pulled a stunt like this with a male tourist. So instead of handing over the money, I began arguing with him in my appallingly fractured Hindi. It went on for several minutes, and it felt like a lot longer. I wasn't sure what I actually said to him, but perhaps my tone said it all. His certainly spoke volumes!

In the end, he agreed to take us back for a mere 20 rupees extra. Hiding my relief, I scrambled back into the scooter with poor Katy, who was badly shaken, deprived of even the limited relief of an adrenaline surge born out of righteous indignation.

In less than 15 minutes, we were back in the blessedly familiar environs of Jorbagh. Our scooter driver drove off in a huff, hurling a few choice swear words in my direction as he went. He had understandably expected a better return on his scam than a measly 20 rupees. But I couldn't have cared less. We were home safely—and surprisingly, the alternating surges of rage and terror, in my case, and unrelieved terror, in Katy's case, had left us ferociously hungry once again, Karim's a distant memory.

Heading for our favorite vegetarian restaurant in nearby Khan Market seemed an apt way for us to celebrate our deliverance, and to detox, as well. The cherry to top off the whipped cream on my delicious vanilla cold coffee drink came in the form of Katy's comment, balm to my injured soul and uttered with unmistakably heartfelt sincerity: "I don't care what anyone says about your Hindi, Farah! That scooter driver certainly understood what you were saying!"

My Breakfast at Tiffany's

by
Elynne Chaplik-Aleskow

Once upon a time, there was a character in a movie who was a free spirit with a love of adventure and life. Her name was Holly Golightly and she was played by the deliciously charismatic Audrey Hepburn. And it was Holly who inspired my secret plan.

This movie had a magical effect on me. I was 16 when I first saw *Breakfast at Tiffany's*. By the time I took my first trip to New York, I had seen the film four times.

Of all the cities I have visited in the world, New York is my most favorite and precious. The city has an infinite rhythm of its own. The opportunities of what to do and see are endless. Day or night one can eat. One can experience any art form. There are always choices for entertainment. The city is alive. It is a life force.

I love the anonymity of New York. I have a need for the

quixotic sensibility, which New York offers me. I am renewed and inspired by my immersion into this city. It is a walking city filled with amazing neighborhoods, quaint groceries, delis, cabarets, music, museums, parks and the ultimate in theater—Broadway.

When attending a Broadway musical, I transcend the reality outside the theater building and am uplifted magically into the all-encompassing talent on stage. The actors play to me beyond their potential to the ultimate of their gifts. The productions are often works of art. To be in a Broadway audience is one of the most satisfying moments of my life. It is for me existence in another dimension.

My first trip to New York was liberating. During the day, I visited Central Park and the pond where Holden Caulfield watched the ducks in *Catcher in the Rye*. I went to New York's museums and walked Fifth Avenue. I played at the FAO Schwarz toy store. I awoke every morning in my own fairytale, waiting to see what the day in this city would offer.

Holly Golightly and I breathed New York in the same way. I inhaled its anticipation, first feeling it in my toes as it worked its way up to my chest and made my brain almost light headed. And tonight was the night I would implement my plan. This was a private plan. I had shared it with no one. It was all mine. I was a romantic and I was fearless.

The theater performance I attended ended around 10:45. I walked through Times Square to one of New York's 24-hour markets and bought doughnuts and milk. Carrying this sweet treasure, I made my way back to my hotel through the exiting theater crowds.

Back in my room, I waited until midnight. With my package

in hand, I headed toward Tiffany's on Fifth Avenue. The door to this jewelry store is recessed. In the darkness of the early morning, I stepped into the doorway and put on my sunglasses that were almost identical to those Audrey Hepburn wore in the movie. I unwrapped my donut, opened my milk and proceeded to have breakfast at Tiffany's.

Suddenly I saw a male figure pass the door in which I was standing. Almost immediately, he slowly walked backward and stopped, staring at me. I could see him more clearly now and realized he was a police officer.

"What are you doing?" he asked in a thick New York accent.

"Having breakfast at Tiffany's, officer," I replied, suddenly feeling very self-conscious.

"Oh, yeah?" he responded, totally unconvinced. "You should know better than to be soliciting here."

"Soliciting?" I repeated. "No, officer, you don't understand. I am having breakfast at Tiffany's. Audrey Hepburn?" I stammered. "The movie?"

He just looked at me and shook his head. "Move on," he said.

Even though the officer had unexpectedly interrupted my fantasy, it did not matter. I had lived it. It was my once-upon-a-time moment.

There's a Small Hotel

by
Nancy Julien Kopp

Our heads were fuzzy and our legs like jelly when we finished the long, overnight flight from Kansas City to Munich, Germany. After clearing passport control and retrieving our luggage, my husband and I headed to the rental car area of the airport. Despite our fatigue, we managed the paperwork and check-out with only a minimum of frustration. An hour later, we settled into a Mercedes C Class sedan and made our way out of the city, Ken at the wheel and map in my hand.

Our next job was to locate the hotel we'd booked on the Internet. I'd searched diligently for a reasonably priced hotel not too far from the Munich airport. I found many, but somehow one kept calling to me, so I clicked and clicked until we were booked for the first three nights of our three-week stay in Germany.

The half-hour drive to Hohenlinden turned into an hour, then another hour. We learned that German roadways are excellent, but that German road signs leave a great deal to be desired. We also discovered that the GPS in our rental car was programmed in German. Useless for us. Round and round we went, on highways and byways, roundabouts and little-traveled pathways. I was near tears and Ken near erupting when we finally pulled into the small rural village of Hohenlinden. Relief was far too mild a word to describe our feelings. Surely the Hotel Zur Linde would soon appear.

"I think it's on the outskirts of the town," I told Ken as he gripped the steering wheel more firmly.

"Not so," he said slowing down in front of a three-story stucco building with "Hotel Zur Linde" painted on the side, right in the middle of town. He pulled into the side drive and around the back to a minuscule parking area, and we walked wearily into the hotel. The small reception area appeared dark and uninviting, but a young girl in the office cubicle smiled and greeted us so warmly that our spirits rose like a hot air balloon on a sunny day.

All we wanted was to go to our room, take a shower and change clothes.

"Oh, I'm so sorry," the young woman said in perfect English. "You cannot go to your room until 2:00. But you can have lunch first." Her smile erased any irritation we might have felt as she led us to the outdoor *biergarten* surrounded by greenery, an arbor and sweet-smelling flowers. *We could easily kill an hour and a half here*, I thought.

A tall glass of the local beer and a bowl of Hungarian soup helped revive us. We lingered in the pleasant outdoor garden until it was time to unload our luggage and take the tiny elevator up to our room. Small, but clean and nicely furnished, the room featured a big window that looked out on a church across the road. The bed, with its snowy white duvet, sheet and soft pillows, looked so inviting.

After showering and changing clothes, we set off on a walk around town. We smiled at the quaint houses, small shops and flower gardens, and our blood pressure cooled back to normal. In one front garden, a man wearing a long cotton coat worked with wood using a standing saw. Ken was thrilled. He told me he'd seen pictures of men doing work like that and wearing the coats to protect their clothes. As we walked, we discussed our plans for the next day, when we would return to the Munich airport to pick up our good friends and traveling partners from South Africa.

In the evening we enjoyed a leisurely and excellent meal in a formal dining room, served by a waitress who had charm plus. Several patrons dined with well-behaved dogs flopped by their feet. The girl who had checked us in that afternoon had left, but her mother was the dining room hostess and hotel clerk for the evening. Mama was tall, slender and blond, wearing spike heels and a low-cut blouse. We chatted with her and were surprised to learn we had booked into a Hungarian hotel. It had good German beer and German food such as roast pork, red cabbage and potato dumplings on the menu, along with a few Hungarian items. Not a problem, especially with the special way we'd been welcomed.

When our waitress brought our meals, she asked what we would say in English to wish someone a good meal. "Enjoy!" I told her, "or even *bon appetit*!" With eyes sparkling, she called out "Enjoy!" as she hurried back to the kitchen. Our food proved to be as satisfying as the hotel itself.

We'd noticed the church across the street filled the summer air with its bells every hour on the hour—lovely bells which chimed for a couple of minutes. We strolled over to the church after dinner and found a small cemetery on one side of the building. Each plot was outlined in paving stones and perennial flowers, some with stone angels adorning the area where the marker sat. We were taken with the care each grave had been given and the gentle, dainty look the flowers and statues added. Hand in hand, we crossed the road to our hotel and bed. "I can't wait to see Mike and Mavis tomorrow," I said to Ken.

At 6 A.M., the church bells began to peal. *Nice*, I thought, as I pulled up the duvet and snuggled deeper into my feather pillow. But the bells went on and on, for 15 minutes. Enough to wake the entire town! Surely, no one in Hohenlinden needed an alarm clock.

After a pleasing breakfast, we zipped into Munich in less than half an hour. Amazing what you can do when you have the proper directions. We picked up our friends at the architecturally impressive airport and brought them to Hotel Zur Linde. Our innkeeper greeted them warmly as new guests—and us as old friends.

"Oh, what a nice place this is," Mavis said, as we helped them to their room down the hall from ours. We met in the biergarten for a tall glass of beer to toast the beginning of our time together. Living halfway across the world from one another, our times together are treasured. We dined outdoors that night, surrounded by locals who ate, chattered and laughed.

We woke up each morning to the 6 o'clock bell concert. By the third morning, I already was awake, looking forward to the chimes, knowing a wonderful German breakfast buffet awaited us. Fresh fruit, cereal, cold meats, cheeses and hard rolls, accompanied by strong coffee and pastries, filled us to satisfaction as we lingered in the sunlit dining room.

Before we checked out, we booked rooms again for our last night in Germany, negotiating a lower price for our return.

After touring the back roads, small towns and villages of southern Germany for three weeks, we returned to Hohenlinden. When we pulled into the parking area, it almost felt like coming home. The four of us strolled into the reception area, and our Hungarian innkeeper came to greet us, 3-inch heels clicking on the tile floor, her face alight with a warm welcome. We definitely were home.

A rainy night meant dinner in the formal dining room with a fire burning to take the chill out of the air. With good food and drink and a chance to recap of all we'd done, we had a lovely final evening in the Hotel Zur Linde.

The next morning, when the church bell concert began, I lay in the comfortable bed, pleased that I'd found this charming small hotel. Or did it find me? With so many choices, why did this one keep calling out to me?

We checked out after breakfast and loaded the car, ready to go to the airport. The four of us made one last trip inside for a warm farewell from the Hungarian hostess of this special hotel. The church bells rang to let us know it was eight o'clock as we drove out of town.

Hotel Zur Linde

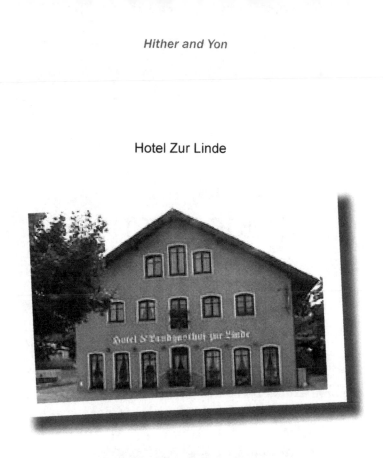

Rhodes Scholar

by
Erika Hoffman

When I travel, I feel proud, at first. I puff up with newly acquired knowledge. Minutes later, I deflate, realizing how ignorant I remain. On a recent cruise originating in Istanbul, Turkey and terminating in Athens, Greece, I experienced many up-and-down moments.

For instance, take Rhodes, Greece. The only factoid about this city I'd retained from my junior high school "daze" was a reference to an ancient colossal statue whose legs once straddled the harbor. The illustration of the Colossus of Rhodes in *Grolier Society's Book of Knowledge* resembled Bruno in *Popeye* cartoon strips, with feet planted on each side of the Aegean inlet. I never gave this Seventh Wonder of the Ancient World any more thought until we pulled into the port.

As I approach my sixth decade, I can verify that knees go first. Helios, the Greek Titan God statue, aka The Colossus of

Rhodes, lasted 65 years before his knees gave way. Then, merchants recycled this 107-foot-high sculpture for scrap parts, which were hauled off to Syria. Helios' sad fate did have a silver lining. When Lady Liberty was built in New York Harbor 2,000 years later, her French creator provided a solid base—so her knees wouldn't buckle!

Gazing at the blue sea, I wondered if the winds had buffeted King Odysseus to Rhodes after his ship got lost returning home from the Trojan War. On second thought, I doubted Homer's hero ever visited this island after the 10-year war in Turkey because the City of Rhodes has always been a bustling place even in ancient times. Back in 280 B.C., Rhodes was a seaport, a shipbuilding town, a stop between the Mideast, Greece and Africa. In *The Odyssey*, King Odysseus ended up mostly on uncivilized atolls populated with pigs and sorceresses and one–eyed monsters. The most entertainment that wayfarer enjoyed was being strapped to the mast of his ship as the sirens sang to him, with their hoping he'd crash his ship up on the rocks.

I sallied off our cruise ship, the *Windstar*, and exuberantly joined my shipmates for a guided tour through Old Town Rhodes.

One bad thing about me as a kid was that I always sat up front near the teacher and asked questions. You've heard that there's no such thing as a dumb question. My teachers assured me they didn't agree. Although time can change monuments, geography and people's appearances, apparently a human's predilection for asking dumb questions stays intact.

I rushed up to stand close to our tour guide. He'd barely

finished telling us about the medieval barrier that surrounded the town, when my arm shot up.

"Certain walls? What does that mean?"

Terry, our own Greek god, cleared his throat. "Curtain walls," he enunciated. "Three and a half miles of sandstone walls surround the palace. Although the Sun God tumbled from earthquakes in 227 B.C., Rhodes still has wonders to offer, like these 20-foot thick walls." He thumped the wall fondly, like an old college buddy. "Folks stood on top and poured burning sand or molten lead down on their enemies' heads when they approached the archway entrances." We all looked upward.

"The Hospitallers who controlled this island during the Middle Ages were members of a religious military society," he confided.

I hung back to whisper to my husband, "Did he say, 'Hospitalists?'" Byron shrugged and took a picture.

"Hospital meant lodging," Terry went on. I suspected this explanation was aimed at me. "The knights were forced to leave the Sovereign Military Hospitaller of St. John of Jerusalem in 1522 when the Turks conquered."

Whenever Terry said the word "Turks," he spat it out. "The knights resettled in Malta."

I piped up. "Are they still in Malta?"

"No, Madame," he said, sighing. "They're in Rome now. Wherever the Turks went, no Christian could remain." He growled, mouthing *Turks*. "And Napoleon captured Malta, so they dispersed."

We'd noticed some big round stone cannon balls, and I

heard Terry mention they could be shot only every few hours. I wondered why but I'd approached my day's quota of stupid questions. Luckily, another dummy asked.

Terry enlightened us. "Cannons have to cool down between shootings. Everything's precise. The *ballistras* are bowed on the side with a canal in the middle. The ball's weight is chiseled on it so the soldiers knew how far each would fly." Terry held his head a little higher as we all oohed and ahhed over Greek ingenuity and superiority.

"For 2,400 years people have trodden these walkways. This is the most modern of European medieval cities," he said, as he pointed to the souvenir shops, craft stores and ceramic ateliers that line the streets. I gazed at the decks of cards displayed in some. They contained illustrations of people entwined in acrobatic sexual positions. Kind of like *Fifty Shades of Grey*, I thought.

Terry described how the people of Rhodes live side by side with history. Every November, they start digging to install cables and sewers and must stop because they always find archeological artifacts. As he spoke, I tried to prepare a question that didn't sound like it came from Beavis or Butthead. Finally, I pontificated on how I'd read about Greek Fire in Steve Berry's thriller *The Venetian Betrayal* and didn't understand what it was. Terry cut me off as I started to divulge the plot.

"Greek Fire's a mixture of sulfur and other things. It's put in ceramic jars and sealed, a wick's added, and then it's thrown at the enemy. Greek Fire was the Byzantine Empire's napalm."

Before I could speak, he continued. "Istanbul was called Byzantium and later Constantinople. The Eastern Roman Empire is the Byzantine Empire where Constantinople had been the capital for over a thousand years."

My head swam like Walt Whitman's. Whitman described the overload on his brain in his poem, *When I Heard the Learned Astronomer Speak*. The poet had to get up and go outside during the scientist's talk and look up "in perfect silence at the stars." Only I couldn't escape, and the hot sun beat down on my bare head. I felt the part in my hair burning—like Greek Fire had been poured over it.

"When the Turks took over, balconies were added and whitewashed. In ancient times there were central sewage systems here!" Terry rattled on.

My lightheadedness didn't prevent me from interrupting. "Really? When we moved to Chatham County, North Carolina, in 1979, outhouses littered the landscape!" He glared at me as if I looked like Medusa, with snakes sprouting out of my head. He signaled the group to follow him.

Terry continued through another hour and several centuries. We finally got up to modern times when Terry pointed out a dedication plaque to Benito Mussolini. Made in 1940, it was one of very few carrying his name. And, it was dated Year 18, because the fascists made up their own calendar and began numbering in 1922.

"I had no idea," I uttered, but by now no one listened to me, and I had even lost my husband in the throng.

Terry launched into a history of the Turks, spitting out every pronunciation of that dreaded name of the people who originally hailed from Mongolia. He pointed to designs in the mosaics that resembled swastikas and explained that a swastika is a symbol of movement, like someone running with two arms and two legs in motion simultaneously.

Finally Terry pointed out the fountains outside of mosques for washing ears, faces, throats, feet and arms. "Leave behind the old; renew yourself," he said. I'd renew myself later with a mojito aboard our ship.

He gave us a final update, but by this time, I'd stopped asking pesky questions. My final notes, scribbled in my moleskin notebook, stained with sweat and smeared ink, was that during WWII the Germans took away adult Jews, but their children stayed. Most left for Israel, so only five Jewish families remain today in Rhodes. Since 10 adult men are needed for a bar mitzvah, they recruit tourists from cruise ships to fill in.

I heard the lovely chirping of birds. Our tour was coming to a close, and I reached into my purse for a tip for our guide.

"Isn't it amazing," I commented, my last insightful observation, "that so many birds thrive within this ancient fortress?" Terry pivoted and pointed toward the source.

"Madame, Serbians sell these bird whistles to kids who love to blow them. It gets to you after a while!" He heaved his chest.

I know Terry will show future amateur Rhodes scholars things I didn't see that day. Because colossal cruise ships churn the waters, discoveries are being dredged up in the harbor every day. Three years ago a fisherman captured a life-sized bronze statue of a woman in his net. Two years ago another farmer on a nearby island found the remains of a temple and 10 statues in a pit.

My discovery? I had learned something new and something unexpected once again. I laughed about my naiveté and bird whistles. Terry cast me a cautious smile.

Once aboard our vessel, I toasted this solidly historic day and the slight diminishment of my ignorance with a mojito.

Erika

CHAPTER EIGHT

Wake-Up Call

Experience is the best teacher.

Of Trust and Travel

by

Samantha Ducloux Waltz

"Dad is actually going to Europe?" My stepdaughter Michele had reason to sound incredulous.

"A bike-and-barge along the Danube in Austria," I said. True, Ray had never been anywhere but Palm Springs, Las Vegas and, oh yes, Maui. But for me—his new wife—he was gathering his courage.

"Can't be too careful," Ray muttered as he packed his wallet and passport into a pouch he'd wear under his clothing. "I've read the warnings in the travel books."

"Gotta run." Michele grabbed the crockpot she'd borrowed. "I don't think Grandpa and Grandma ever traveled, either. Good luck."

I turned to Ray. "You'll be fine. Europe is a lot like the United States."

He threw me a yeah-right look. "Pickpockets everywhere.

Scammers at the train station. I've heard stories."

Courage, man, I wanted to say, but didn't. This was not his finest hour.

When I'd met Ray, we had a thousand things in common. Both of us enjoyed hiking, biking and skiing, held season tickets to the Oregon Symphony, and treasured our teenage children. He was kind and gentle with a quirky sense of humor. I immediately fell deeply, madly in love. I'd traveled widely and I found going to new places and meeting new people to be as essential as breathing. He hadn't, and didn't. Apparently fear of the unknown was genetic. But I longed to explore the world with him.

Not that I think a wife's job is to change her husband. A big part of any relationship is acceptance. Nor am I saying that there is nothing of merit to enjoy in Palm Springs, Las Vegas or Maui—especially Maui—with its fabulous snorkeling. But traveling beyond our borders gives us powerful insights about both our own country and others. One can't visit the Mayan ruins at Tulum without marveling at the achievements of a culture lacking in the technologies we consider so necessary. Or confront the poverty of Calcutta without gasping at the luxury most of us consider a standard middle-class life in the United States. Secretly, I hoped this bike-and-barge vacation would be the first of many trips with Ray.

"You have your money belt?" Ray asked. "Have to be especially careful in the big cities. We'll be spending four days in Vienna."

Vienna, I thought. *Baroque splendors. Lipizzaner stallions performing the Grand Quadrille. Schubert and Haydn.*

Then I imagined what Ray was thinking. *Vienna. Foreigners. Thieves.*

The bike-and-barge proved delightful, and Ray relaxed a little more each day as we pedaled through picturesque villages, dismounting long enough to wander through Baroque churches and buy bread and cheese at local shops.

As the days passed, he was more and more the warm, enthusiastic companion I so loved. We were both enchanted by the ethereal sound of the Vienna Boys' Choir, the jeweled splendor of the Imperial Treasury at the Hofburg Palace and the historical ambience of the Schönbrunn Palace. Still, I sensed Ray kept up his guard.

Our third day in Vienna, as we stood on a bridge overlooking the Danube, the sun broke through a lightly overcast sky and scattered silver on the water. "Aren't you glad we came?" I murmured.

"So far," he said carefully. "My parents missed a lot by not traveling."

I curled my fingers into his, feeling like the luckiest girl in the world, as we walked back to our hotel. But when we stepped into the small lobby of Hotel Tabor, our hotel clerk stepped forward and greeted us with the question that causes every tourist to quake. "Did you by chance lose your wallet?" he asked.

Ray stiffened and audibly inhaled.

"Non." I shook my head confidently as I touched the pouch at my waist, its familiar bulge reassuring me. I knew Ray's wallet was zipped into his money belt, as well.

The color drained from Ray's face as he patted his money

belt, his right pants pocket, and then his left. "My wallet is gone." His voice was almost a whisper, and his eyes widened with panic. "How will we get home? We should never have come."

My heart rose in my throat. *How could anyone get at Ray's wallet?* I wondered. I'd never had something like this happen during my travels. There would be the trouble of notifying our bank and canceling our credit cards, of course. But worse— he'd nix future trips.

"Perhaps this is it." The clerk's usually impassive face broke into a broad smile. With the flourish of a magician pulling a rabbit from a hat, he drew a wallet from under the counter and set it before us.

"Everything's gone. I know it," Ray muttered as he gingerly picked it up. I hardly breathed as he thumbed through its contents. He checked it a second time, and a third. "It's all here," he said, his voice filled with the wonder of a child at Christmas.

My knees nearly buckled with relief. "How did you get it?" I asked the clerk.

Still grinning, he handed Ray a piece of paper. "The person who returned it left his name and number."

I called the second we got to our room.

"Hallo, Roland hier," a young man answered.

In the little German I knew, I thanked him. "Guten tag. Vielen dank."

"It was nothing," he said in careful English and explained how he and his girlfriend, Steffi, found the wallet on the ground near an outside table at McDonald's. They studied the picture on Ray's driver's license and then put the wallet on an empty table nearby while they ate lunch, watching to see if someone who looked like Ray would come for it. When no one did, he and Steffi thumbed through the contents, found a receipt from our hotel, and returned the wallet.

As I listened, I could picture the event clearly. Ray had stopped at the McDonald's near St. Stephens for a frozen yogurt and a comfortable touch of home while I checked emails at a nearby cyber café. He would have pulled out his wallet to pay for the yogurt and dropped it there. Roland and Steffi, spotting it, could easily have taken the money and credit cards, justifying Ray's suspicion of foreigners that the past two weeks had nearly put to rest. Or, if too honest for that, the young couple could have simply handed the wallet to a McDonald's employee. Instead, they made the 20-minute walk to our hotel to return it, contents intact. So much time for someone to take for strangers.

"We think what you've done is amazing. We want to reward you," I told Roland.

"Insist," Ray coached me.

"No, please. It was our pleasure," Roland said.

We chatted a few more minutes, exchanging email addresses. I made a mental note to send Steffi and Roland a coffee table book of Oregon when we got home. If I'd had a crystal ball, I would have seen future years of their visits to us in Oregon and our visits with them and their families in Graffenbach, Lower Austria and Mökriach, Carinthia, and then meeting them in Paris and again in London. But for the moment, I could see only Ray's face with a smile lighting his eyes and curving his lips.

"There are good people everywhere," Ray said when I hung up. "I never knew. Maybe we could invite them to stay with us in Oregon. Show them around."

I agreed. We could take them somewhere completely different from their lush, green country. *Oh, I had it.* I laughed to myself. *Maybe Palm Springs or Las Vegas? Or, hey, as a thank you for opening the world to Ray, maybe we could even find a way to take them to Maui.*

Left to right: Ray and Samantha Waltz, Roland Holzbauer (back), Stefanie "Steffie" Starz, Dorothy Manfull, Walter Holzbauer and Robert Manfull.

Imperial Benediction

by
Sarah Chrisman

I watched the omnipresent advertisements and electronic distractions increase in frequency and sheer, oppressive clutter as the train neared Tokyo's center. Or, rather, what passes for a center in that massive urban nightmare that sprawls, gray and dirty white, like some huge bird's droppings over the alluvial plain. I was rapidly approaching the place where the emperor's palace was located, so I suppose it laid greater claim to the term "center" than any other given point in that bloated metropolis.

I had come to Japan with *samisen* music ringing in my ears, my bags heavy with histories of *geisha*, and a contract for more money than I had seen in my life carefully snuggled next to the visa in my passport. I would lay my bare feet upon tatamis in castles built by shoguns, sip tea prepared in sacred ceremonies while gazing on carefully sculpted gardens of great antiquity. The people were a race of honor, who valued their traditions and eschewed short-term expediencies—was not this the very nation that had created the Kyoto Accords? Pure souls and crystal air awaited me.

Reality can sometimes interrupt our dreams with the shocking force of a bucket of Sapporo beer emptied into the middle of a Zen garden. The lucrative contract on which I had laid the foundations of so many dreams proved so riddled with loopholes and fine print revealed upon landing that after all factors were considered and the exchange rate figured in, I was left with barely more than a living wage.

The castles were concrete replicas younger than I was, and tea was mostly something in a plastic bottle grabbed from a hot case in the convenience store. As for the clean air accords, observation had forced me to conclude Kyoto had offered a sale on convention space that year—if the massive piles of perfectly recyclable white paper piled in "burnables" trash bins and headed for incineration had not led me to this belief, the smoggy grit of the air undoubtedly would have done so.

By the end of the first month, my spirits had sunk to depths usually only seen by the oddest of ocean-dwelling biology, and my bank account was emaciated. Nevertheless, I had scraped together enough funds for a brief trip to Tokyo for the New Year's holiday. I had heard that January 2nd was the one day of the year when the emperor of Japan made a public appearance. So many other representations of classical Japan had proven themselves concrete illusions—I was determined to pursue this golden reality.

Stepping out of the station after the long, slow train ride, I followed the directions of a tiny policeman herding tourists like cattle. Russians, Americans—I hadn't seen this many *gaijin* in one place since I'd left Seattle. My heart might have fallen a little when I saw how many fair heads there were in the line to see the emperor. I was not then so unique in my quest for that elusive glimpse of the past. Just one out of a thronging hoard, lining up to see the spectacle.

Something seemed to pass through the crowd after security had been cleared and we moved over the Nijubashi Bridge—the most well-known bridge in Japan. It marked the entrance to the palace grounds and only felt the feet of ordinary mortals on this and one other day each year. A hush rippled through the crowd, as though we were entering a great cathedral open to the sky, and excitement grew. Wave upon wave of us flooded around the base of the palace, all eyes turned upward toward a glass-walled balcony with a backdrop of golden rice-paper screens.

Then He came, moving from behind those elegant screens and smiling, welcoming, the direct descendant of the sun goddess Amaterasu Ōmikami, highest amongst the heavens—his imperial majesty, emperor of the islands of Japan. Following and flanking him came his family, heirs to the world's oldest unbroken monarchial line, striding with the dignity of millennia of tradition. They smiled upon us, and waved, and the crowd exploded.

"Banzai! BANZAI! BANZAIIII!!" A small man screamed next to me, all the force of his lungs ushered into that imperial benediction, "May you live a thousand years."

They were cheering, they were shouting, and everywhere flags were waving. I was waving my flag, too, madly flapping and fluttering that small banner of red and white with the wild vigor of the awe-struck, and I did not notice until later that I'd torn it. A couple of thousand years passed in a few minutes, and they were gone, moving back into their tiled palace behind those shoji screens of sun-flecked gold. We crowds moved away, granting them peace as they had given us joy. I dropped my torn flag into a pile where someone was collecting them, with a slight regret that it was spoiled past keeping.

My mind was dancing with the joy of those crowds as I went back to the train station, standing among the rush of dark heads where I'd promised to meet a friend. From out of those hurrying throngs stepped a man, the tallest Japanese man I had ever seen, with ramrod posture and a warrior's step. He carried a walking stick carved into the form of a *katana*, its end wrapped around in silk like the hilts of those old, perfect swords. But this staff could not possibly be to aid in walking. There was no trace of falter in his gait, no hesitation in the strength of his legs as, looking neither left nor right, he strode directly toward me, his eyes holding mine. I looked behind me, sure he must be meeting someone else, for who was I to this regal man? There was no one else. I stood alone in my own private circle.

He stopped the distance of a sword-strike away from me, and bowed in a swift, graceful motion which I could never replicate, though I tried, with utmost respect. "Konnichiwa." I smiled, uncertain what was expected of me.

He caught my eyes, and held them. "Watashiha, samurai desu." He touched the walking stick that looked so much like a scabbarded katana, held it up so that I was sure to understand. "Watashiha, samurai desu." I am a samurai, in Japanese.

He gave me a flag, just like the one I had torn, but inscribed with calligraphy in a style so old that none of the Japanese friends I later questioned could even read, let alone translate, it. Then he was gone, striding along his own magically clear path through the crowds and out into the brilliant sun of a festival day.

Somewhere, deep within myself, I felt the refrains of samisen music.

Top: Sarah listens to instructions before entering the grounds of the Imperial Palace.

Bottom: Palace statue of a Samurai warrior

Celebrating Saint Somebody

by

Todd McGough

Navigating Managua's *Mercado Huembes* was not easy. In addition to being a sprawling collection of stalls that sold everything from cigars to chickens, it was also the hub for all buses headed for southern Nicaragua.

I was headed for the wharf at San Jorge on Lake Nicaragua. At times like this, I really felt my 58-plus years. It was 9:30 in the morning and already hot. I was sweating profusely. Squeezing sideways between barbequing meat and music CD vendors, I scanned the bus terminal area, looking for someone in charge to ask about buses heading south. Suddenly, several men in sweat-stained shirts called out to me, "Frontera! San Juan Del Sur!" A stranger stepped toward me with outstretched arms in an attempt to relieve me of my backpack, an offer I declined. "San Jorge," I told the man I guessed to be the boss, the *jefe*. He nodded at a bus just next to where we were standing. I wrestled my backpack aboard and settled in.

The bus's engine stirred to life and lurched into Managua's rush hour traffic. Clearing the city's center, the bus found its purpose and jostled southward. Over the next few hours, we moved through a chain of cities and greenscapes: the smoldering Volcano Mombacho, the arts center of Masaya, the turnoff for Colonial Granada. One of the men I recognized from the terminal collected our fares.

Eventually the bus gasped and pulled over. My seat-neighbor motioned to me that this was my stop, so I stepped off the bus, into the hot sun, and then into a taxi. Fifteen minutes later, I was standing at the foot of an ancient concrete pier where a ferry was disgorging a mixed load of local Nica families and assorted backpackers. On the horizon to the east, I saw the looming twin peaks of Ometepe. There was an information booth where a man with a pencil-thin mustache handed me a brochure and told me about the place to stay in Moyogalpa, which was the main town on Ometepe Island. I took it and moved on.

The last thing you want to happen in Latin America is be left standing on a trip of any kind, so my traveler's instinct told me to get on board the ferry early. I crossed a rickety gangplank and went below to weigh the advantages of the various seats. The bobbing ship looked like an anemic version of the "little tugboat that could." Upstairs was a wheelhouse with several benches, and a seating area below with more benches. The deck was a patchwork of plywood, with water sloshing about underneath. *No snack bar here*, I thought to myself as passengers quickly filled the boat.

After an hour of wobbling and sloshing, the boat approached the harbor at Moyogalpa. The nearest volcanic peak was now towering above me. After the boat docked, I collected my things and disembarked.

As with every place in Nicaragua, there are people waiting to sell, transport, help and hustle you. It's the way of life for Nicas who live anywhere near a tourist destination. Some of the passengers climbed into marked vans, while others followed the local kids who urged them along. Backpackers, decked out in brand new gear, straggled up the street with their noses buried in copies of *Lonely Planet*.

I set off for the Hotel Aly at the recommendation of the man with the pencil mustache. Finding the place, I was pleasantly surprised. It appeared clean and had an attractive, well-landscaped lounge and dining area. The rooms were stark: a bed, nightstand and fan. And the price was right. I slung my backpack onto the bed and sighed the sigh of relief that comes at the end of a long day of travel. It was now three in the afternoon.

Walking around a new town is a kind of psychological need for me. It's as if I have to experience it as a concrete object before I can accept that it exists. I walked to the end of the main street and looked both ways. Moyogalpa was a small town, very small—maybe six blocks of paved streets and then dirt roads. There was the plaza, the church and a small tienda selling everything from rope to milk. I saw festive flags and many people on horseback. I then noticed the malodorous funk that seemed to follow me, so I headed back to Hotel Aly for a badly needed shower.

Upstairs, I stepped gamely into the shower then girded

myself for the expectant gush of cool water—there was no hot water here. I turned the knob and barely a trickle exited. The empty pipe peered back at me. *Uh, oh. No water? That's not good.* I could put up with many things, but no water—that was a hygiene issue. Downstairs, management acted puzzled. "Really? No water? It should be back on in a little while," they assured me.

Others were not sure. I went into the restaurant and a woman there said the water was supposed to be out for three days. Then she shared that it was a holiday weekend and a huge party would occur that very night. Who knew?

There are times when patience alone will suffice, and this was one of them. I ordered a melon and pineapple smoothie. *Ahhhh. Man, that's good.* Smoothies in the U.S. don't seem to have the same flavor or texture. To kill time, I checked my email and nosed around the lobby. I looked at a large map of the island hanging on the wall.

"Can you go all the way around Ometepe by bus?" I asked the old man at the front desk. Suddenly, I heard something. It was running water! I dashed upstairs and saw water coming from my shower pipe. Not a flood or a steady flow, but a healthy trickle, enough for knocking off a few layers of Nicaraguan road crud.

Later, from my window I heard the sound of a party. I looked, but only heard loud popping noises, unable to quite locate them in the pre-sunset glow. After a few minutes, I saw the flash of light, and a split second later, a loud pop, announcing the start of the celebration of Saint Somebody.

I ascended to the hotel's balcony. Surprised that no one

else joined me, I soon realized I had the best seat in town. Before me, a parade was stirring to life. Over the next hour, the parade unfolded below: dance troupes, cowboys and cowgirls on horseback and more dancers. And then the piece de resistance—the likeness of Saint Somebody came into view, borne on the shoulders of four women walking in cadence. The whole town roared to a fevered pitch. Two guys with giant skyrockets ignited their fireworks, sending them high into the night sky.

As the parade headed up the street, it was framed by the huge emerald volcano. The moon rose in the darkening sky and was soon streaked silver from the skyrockets. Right then, I had an *ahhhhaaaa* experience that comes from the perfect moment. Suddenly it was all so clear: *This is why I came. This is why I love to travel.*

Such moments are rare in a lifetime, especially in places that seem to esteem permits and paperwork—over what? It's hard to say what it is—perhaps the unfiltered view of the human condition. I can sense when it happens and respond deeply to it. But it can't be explained. That's why I'll be back, soon enough.

Todd surfs every day in Nicaragua, when he's not teaching English at the University of Leon.

Welcome to Cameroon!

by
Eldon Dale

In my humble opinion, there are three kinds of travelers:

A. The cruise-and-be-waited-on traveler
B. The see-the-mega-sites-of-the-world traveler
C. All the others

Having done both A and B, letter C is where it is at for me these days. I have traveled to 80 countries. Favorites? The people, the tribes and the primitive customs I have witnessed in 11 African nations have been, by far, my best travel adventures. But there are some places in the world you just don't need to go, and Cameroon is number one on that list.

Sitting on the central western coast of the African continent just above the equator and next to Nigeria, Cameroon's rich, forested lands spread throughout its 183,560 square miles. Its 19 million citizens speak French, plus their tribal languages. The country claims to be officially the Republic of

Cameroon, but our guides shared that it was the most corrupt country in Africa. We didn't doubt them! When we visited the country in 2000, we witnessed the forests being demolished by French logging trucks—a huge oil pipeline was being built through the northern section of the country. And we soon learned the country was just not ready for tourists.

But I'm getting ahead of myself. In the beginning, our long-time traveling buddy, Carole, presented the trip idea to my wife and me. She said it would be a private tour in a West African country where we could visit the pygmies—the Bayak tribe—and also observe lowland gorillas in the wild. It sounded good to us, so we agreed. When all was said and done and the trip planned and paid for, our traveling group consisted of adventurous me; Janis, my good-natured wife; Carole, the no-fear instigator of off-the-wall travel adventures; Wanda, the Hollywood voodoo priestess; and Henry. I will tell you more about Henry later.

Five travelers, two drivers, one guide and two Land Cruisers—we were ready for adventure! Our first stop in Cameroon was in a parking lot, where the requisite welcoming dance was presented. The local Juju dance required traveler participation, of course. Dancing with them, I knew I impressed the natives with my '60s Watutsi moves when they suddenly released a bag of snakes! I immediately started doing the Surfer Stomp. Little did our hosts know that I have been dubbed "Indiana Jones" by my kids—both of us adventurers share the same feelings about snakes. Welcome to Cameroon!

Later, after surviving the surprise snake dance, I had a bad feeling after seeing grease dripping from both front ends of our vehicles and voiced my concern to our two guides. "No problem," said one. "These are our cars and we take good care of them." I was hesitant, but took them for their word, knowing the four-wheeled Land Cruisers were good cars since I owned one myself.

The roads outside the capital city of Yaoundé consisted of a red clay dust with a washboard surface. To our collective dismay, the drivers felt compelled to use the four-wheel drive option—until the wheel bearings started smoking. It was then we heard them say that the car rental agency was not going to be happy! But we pushed on, only slowing down from our race-car speed to leave guards special tokens of appreciation for examining our passports at security huts along the road. Bring it on, Cameroon!

We arrived at a small town and our tent camp where we would depart the next day to see the gorillas. That afternoon, our small troop ventured off into the jungle to see the Pygmy people, one of the two promised highlights of our trip. The group of very short men, women and children were surprised to see us, but cordial. Their huts were made from palm fronds, and the kids ran in and out of them, dressed in donated Western-style clothing.

The elder leader offered to show us an authentic Bayak dance and having seen other African tribes perform wonderful dances, we watched in great anticipation as the drums started. The leader stood as tall as he could—about four feet in all—put his hands out in front of him, and moved his feet slowly back and forth. That was it. Seriously. The dance lasted all of 20 seconds. The five of us stood there in shocked silence, thinking he would continue, but he was done and looked at us for approval. All we could do was clap in utter amazement. We had paid a lot of money and had traveled to this remote country to see the Pygmy people, and, needless to say, were a touch disappointed. But I do demonstrate this "pygmy shuffle" for my friends. I learned to dance like a Pygmy, all 5 feet, 9 inches of me. When in Rome, ah, I mean, Cameroon.

Back at camp, we encountered more surprises. From firsthand experience, I can say with authority that tent camping in Africa is fun. But Cameroon topped it all, and not in a good way: the large furry animal that came through the rip in the wall of the tent and landed on my wife's cot in the middle of the night made things really exciting. Apparently, it was just as shocked as my wife and left through the rip in a big hurry. The wonders of Cameroon!

Finally, the day came, and we were off to see the promised elusive, lowland gorillas. The girls rode in the car with the air conditioning, while Henry and I rode in the car without air conditioning. This meant having the windows down for the entire trip, and as such, all of the red road dust joined us inside the car. I wore a bandana over my mouth, donned sunglasses to protect my eyes, turned my collar up to ward off the dust, and positioned my ball cap backward on my head. And last, I shoved Kleenex up my nostrils. Needless to say, my attempt to keep the dust out was futile, as it found its way into every nook and cranny of my body!

We traveled by car as far as the road could go into the jungle, and then continued on foot. Together, the five of us—Janis, Carol, Henry, Wanda and I—along with our guide and two teenage town boys who carried packs and supplies "Buwana style" on their heads, walked several hours until we came upon a clearing near a watering hole. We were near the eastern border of Cameroon and the Central African Republic (CAR). The plan was to spend two nights there, on the border, in a tree house situated 30 feet above the ground, viewing gorillas, elephants and other wild creatures. After that, we would cross over by foot into CAR to see more wildlife and gorillas, as well.

We got settled into the tree house, arranged our mosquito netting, and the women set out a special container for nighttime usage. All of us watched diligently for any wildlife as the sun started to set, but nothing appeared. After the guide and his boys set up their camp, the guide came to us with the good news, and yes, I'm being sarcastic—he had neglected to pack food for our stay! It was a good thing we had brought along water, beef jerky, nuts and candy for snacks. *Survivor: Cameroon!*

Throughout the night, we waited patiently for those elusive gorillas. Nothing. We learned later that the dozens of French logging trucks we had seen hauling lumber out of the forest had sent the gorillas across the border into CAR. And we also learned that day that because CAR was involved in a political coup and their President had fled into Cameroon, our trip into the CAR was canceled! All was not lost, though—the dead jungle silence was broken at dawn by three ducks. It was just a very long way to go to see three ducks. Being the good sports we were, when our guide returned in the morning, we told him, "Get us the hell out of here!" Time to leave Cameroon!

Trust me, it gets better. While hiking out of the jungle in the heat and humidity, Carole collapsed. We suspected heat stroke and checked her supplies for water. That's when we learned the teen French-speaking porters were only carrying Carole's supply of Diet Dr. Pepper. She had no water. Our guide decided to go ahead to warn the drivers we were leaving earlier than planned and left us alone with the teens and an ailing Carole. With the three of us watching—Janis, Henry and myself—the Hollywood Priestess decided to meditate Carole back to health and started chanting about waterfalls or something. Being of a more practical persuasion, I finally got Carole to eat some salt and sugar and drink some of our water. We abandoned the search for stretcher parts when Carole finally responded and was able to walk again. Our ragtag group—sans our guide—found its way out of the jungle and back to the drop-off point, where we waited several hours for the drivers and our guide. Not exactly what we planned to do in Cameroon!

We found a decent hotel in that little town where we started, and after cleaning up the best we could—I took a shower in my clothes since there wasn't a laundry anywhere nearby, and then showered again in the buff to try and get the incessant dust off—we all went to dinner. We were famished! By then, it was past the usual dining time, but the waiter said he would serve us. We tried ordering some simple, easily prepared items, but the waiter returned from the kitchen saying the cook did not want to cook those items.

After three attempts, I asked if the cook had bread. "Yes." Did he have cheese? "Yes." Could he put the cheese on the bread and grill it? "Yes." Our sandwiches came, but the cheese smelled like rotten goat cheese! Our High Priestess decided to talk to the cook and left for the kitchen. When she returned, she informed us that the waiter was the cook! So much for dinner. Ahh, starving in Cameroon!

After convincing our guide to return us to the capital, we contacted the local travel agent and arranged to leave Cameroon, cutting our adventure short about a week. Enough of Cameroon!

Now, time to tell you about Henry. Henry was an 82-year-old excommunicated Catholic priest. A professor of literature at a prestigious East Coast university, Henry was a world traveler, having visited 175 countries. Eccentric, intelligent and educated, Henry was also a man of few words. But when he said to me, "This is the worst f_ _king trip I have ever taken," I had to agree.

Goodbye and good riddance to Cameroon!

Top: Eldon doing the snake dance with natives.

Bottom: Portrait of Eldon and dirt.

Aloha Spirit Revisited

by
John J. Lesjack

There used to be an old Hawaiian man living on the windward side of Oahu near Ka'a'awa. His ancient farmhouse sat just far enough up the sloping hillside so that the muted roar of the ocean rolled along green pastures, through eucalyptus trees, over recumbent branches and right into his living room. Behind his house, he had a sort of carport or shed, jammed with a tractor and other farm implements. Did he grow taro, sweet potatoes, bananas? I never knew. What I did know was that he was kind to me before I ever set foot on his red soil.

He wore work clothes and a wide-brimmed hat and looked like he could have stepped right onto the set of Twentieth Century Fox during the filming of *South Pacific*. But it wasn't his clothing that I remember most. It was his attitude of welcome. He smiled with his whole body as he watched two cars—one person in each car—escorted by an old gray dog, rolling up his rutted driveway past rows of leafy foliage. He watched as both cars stopped in front of his shed.

This was in March 1956, and the farmer was transfixed and confused by people arriving on a Saturday for no special occasion—no luau, no birthday celebration, no planned socializing of any kind. His son—my shipmate—had overheard me talking in the chow line about my concern for my car. The son volunteered the shed on his father's farm and then called home to say we were driving over from Pearl Harbor to drop off my car before our ship left for the Marshall Islands. We would be gone eight months.

I wish I had taken a picture of that man and his son, standing there in a slight breeze, while a surrealistic light fog moved past them. The farmer stared into his son's brown eyes with pride as his son stood tall in his dress blues, shined shoes and military bearing. At the least, I wish I had photographed that old farm house in front of the glistening Ko'olau Mountains. My friend went inside the house to say goodbye to his mother. We soon heard her crying. What I did was acquaint myself with the farmer, and then casually asked about storage space for my car.

We put my Ford in the shed and covered it with canvas. The three of us then climbed into my friend's car, and with his father driving and his dog taking point in front of the car, we caravanned down the driveway. I thanked the dog from the back seat before we turned onto the highway and traveled back to the main gate of Pearl Harbor, Territory of Hawaii. The farmer returned home in his son's car.

That fall in Honolulu I hitched a ride with tourists from

Indiana who cautiously navigated the curves of the Old Pali Road, which was built in 1932. At the top of the Nuʻnanu Pali—1,200 feet above sea level—the strong winds troubled the Hoosiers who preferred the safer leeward side of Oahu. When they turned around, I exited their car. While I waited for another ride, I listened to the winds singing and enjoyed a pure, unadulterated natural view of Kāneʻohe Bay. Water colors, changing from blue to turquoise and in between, unfolded before me. Having seen the *USS Arizona* smokestacks earlier that day, and conscious that ancient warriors had once died in battle in this high place, I thought, *Graveyard at the bottom of Pearl Harbor and graveyard near the top of the Pali—graveyards above and below the sea.*

An older couple from Wisconsin—at age 19, everyone was older than I was—picked me up and navigated the road down the Pali as I told my story. They listened to me explain how I was going to pick up my 1940 Ford convertible, a car I had not seen for eight months due to my Marshall Islands tour. I told them that the car was stored on my friend's father's farm, and that my friend and I were *ohuna*, Hawaiian for family, because once on board the same ship, we were all family. I didn't have his dad's address, but I remembered the area. By late afternoon, after checking several mom-and-pop grocery stores, the tourists dropped me off at the end of the rutted driveway.

I had barely begun to walk on the red soil when the old dog came out to say *aloha*. Walking on land and enjoying the scent of flowers, I let the quietness take me. Was I drawn to the peacefulness of that farm? Or was it just the car I wanted? I didn't know. My eyes took in the land, the sky and the mountains, and I understood why Hawaiians believed that everything, even their red soil, contained divine power, or *mana*. As the softness of the farm's surroundings washed over me, I was reminded of the time I heard a man say, "On my father's farm, heaven was a local call." On this farm, heaven was also a local call.

The farmer acted as if he had expected me. His wife called to me from the house and graciously invited me to stay for tea. I apologized for having to decline. I had been given a brief liberty to obtain my car and had to return to the ship that evening. I recalled feeling that those two Hawaiians had personally put the grace in gracious.

The farmer and I walked out to the shed where I had left my car. When I saw that the shed was empty, my heart sank. That 1940 Ford had cost me four paychecks and it was my first convertible. I had planned to sell it for what I paid for it because I needed the money for college after the Navy. But at that moment my greatest concern was how I would get back to my ship. Being AWOL in 1956 meant brig time.

The farmer misunderstood my distress and became very humble, or *ha'aha'a*. He apologized for having driven my car into town and for having parked my car two stalls over from where I had left it. He was quick to point out that he had filled the gas tank for me. He and his wife had never ridden in a convertible and had wanted to see what riding in one was like. He hoped that I didn't mind he had driven my car.

I was relieved that I wasn't going to the brig, but I didn't know how to apologize in Hawaiian. The truth was that I felt blessed by knowing the farmer and his son. Had my car been left on the docks in the shipyard, it would have been stolen or towed. People doing a kindness without being attached to the outcome—the Hawaiian language with words like *mahalo* for gratitude—and this manifestation of Aloha Spirit were all strange to me. And now the farmer was worried about how I felt about him using the car for a little joy ride with his wife.

"Mahalo," I said many times, hoping I communicated to the farmer how grateful I was for what he had done for me and that I was happy he and his wife had enjoyed the car.

"Was the sun shining during your little excursion?" I asked him.

"Yes, yes," he said. "We went to the beach."

"Good," I said. "Very good."

What was the Hawaiian word for "good," I wondered.

I had another surprise. When we removed the tarp covering the car, we exposed a very clean little Ford. Not only had the farmer started the car once a week to keep the battery up, he had wiped the car off on a regular basis. I was astounded. "Mahalo," I said again. "Mahalo."

The top was up, the back window zippered into place, and the keys in the ignition, exactly where I had left them. I fussed over the cleanliness of the car and communicated some positive energy about how happy I was with everything and how blessed I felt.

"Mahalo," I said. The farmer then bowed to me. Out of respect, I bowed to him. Could a Midwesterner bow appropriately? I hoped so.

I tried to take out my wallet to pay him, tried to give him some money, offered to give him a ride into town, offered to come out and work for him. He refused everything. The Aloha Spirit, I learned later, cannot be bought, sold or traded. It isn't measured by money or words, but by actions and lasting gestures.

The farmer and I shook hands solemnly and said, "Aloha." When I mentioned his son, the farmer said his son had been transferred to Japan while I was back on the mainland. The son was most happy in Japan.

My car started up easily. I rolled the window down, shifted into reverse, backed out of the shed, put the car in first gear, and waved goodbye. The farmer, joined by his wife who was wiping her hands on her apron, waved back. Their old dog did his job and escorted me down to the end of the driveway. I thanked him and turned right. I drove into a slight fog and out of that farmer's life before I cranked up my window.

That farm couple's generosity has never left me. Their son's magnanimous gesture of goodwill is one of my finest memories. We are still ohuna in my mind, and their energy is still with me, yes, but I regret to say not their names. Out of respect, I choose to not substitute other names for the real ones. But the story doesn't end there.

That famous Hawaiian entertainer Don Ho once said, "We don't realize as the years go by the place we grew up in doesn't stay the same."

In June of 1998 I returned to Oahu with my 22-year-old daughter and met the trade winds again as one meets an old and cherished friend. I had returned because I had been away so long I couldn't remember the place anymore. And, secretly, I hoped to say thank you to my old shipmate from the *USS Lipan ATF 85*.

In the spirit of the islands, my daughter and I did not rent a convertible. For our three days on Oahu, we rented a Jeep. We didn't put the top down. We removed it and, with my daughter driving, headed for the windward side of the island.

Don Ho was absolutely right. The place where one grows up doesn't stay the same.

Three highways and three tunnels now connected the leeward with the windward sides of the island. I had known only one highway and no tunnels. The Pali Highway took us to the Naʻuanu Pali State Park exit where we stopped for the view. Kāneʻohe Bay was right where I had left it. Cumulus clouds and mists were scudding majestically along but the highway on the windward side was straight and smooth. We looked down on a golf course and country club. The number of buildings had increased on the windward side but the slopes were still covered with greenery and the Koʻolau Mountains were still dripping water. Thousands of bones had been discovered during construction of the new road and reportedly were stored in a museum.

We had three days on Oahu, but how much time would we need to reconnect with a person, a place and an experience remembered from the 1950s? More than three days. I didn't find the man. What's the Hawaiian word for "regret?"

I was on my way home from work recently when I saw a garage sale sign that led to some women by the side of the road. I bought an imitation Hawaiian gourd called *ipu*. I was drawn to the replica because of its sign, "Aloha Inspiration Jar." Shell beads lined the neck of the ipu. A cork stopper was in the top of the jar and the cork attached to a string. The jar itself was filled with wooden beads and inside each bead was an ancient Hawaiian saying or bit of wisdom.

I removed the cork and took out one bead. I removed the folded paper from the bead and read a section of Hawaiian wisdom that spoke to me.

I kahi 'e no ke kumu mokihana, paoa 'e no 'one'I I ke 'ala.

Translation: Although the mokihana tree is at a distance, its fragrance reaches here.

John's daughter, Sierra, at the wheel.

The Potties of Guate

by
Pat Nelson

When I embarked for Guatemala a few years ago, I thought I understood bathroom etiquette for travel in Latin America. I knew that to find a restroom I should say *baño* or *sanitario*. With those two handy words in my vocabulary, I felt prepared for the trip, certain I wouldn't get caught with my pants down.

A friend met me at noon at Guatemala City's La Aurora International Airport. He had warned me that it might not be safe to arrive after dark. My first stop was the airport baño, which held no surprises. It was a clean American-style restroom with plenty of paper, both toilet tissue and towels. There was hot and cold running water and a sparkling mirror on the wall. The only thing missing was a toilet seat, a common omission in Mexico, as well. I wondered why. Did it solve the dilemma of whether to leave the seat up or down, or make cleaning easier, or help people develop strong leg muscles from hovering without soiling one's shoes?

We headed for the bus station for a five-hour bus ride and one-hour taxi ride to my friend's home at Quilinco, in the western Guatemalan highlands. After he purchased bus tickets and checked the luggage, we had just enough time to walk down the street for a quick lunch of chewy *carne asada* with rice and salad.

In preparation for the long bus ride, I visited a room marked *damas*—for women. A group of men at a nearby table watched as I opened the door. Water covered the floor of the tiny room. A plastic bucket of water in the sink caught the stream from the faucet before it drained into the lake on the floor. I backed out and walked past the grinning men. Just as well. I'd forgotten to stuff my pockets with toilet tissue at the airport or to bring napkins from the restaurant table, and the bathroom was not stocked with paper.

After lunch, we started the long bus ride to Huehu-etenango, called Huehue (pronounced *way way*) for short. I should have used the soppy restroom at the restaurant since there was no baño on the bus. We sat in the very back where a bathroom had once been—the company had no doubt found it to be more profitable to add five more seats across the back of the bus instead. During the long ride, the Guatemalans seemed to be skilled at holding it—no one asked the driver to stop.

Halfway through the trip, after two and a half hours of climbing higher and higher on paved but bumpy and curvy roads, we stopped for a 10-minute break. I was relieved to see the sign *sanitarias damas*, but I wasn't fast enough so ended up far back in the line of women. No men stood next door at *sanitarios caballeros*. All had walked directly to the edge of the ravine and in full view of everyone had relieved themselves. I was glad I hadn't walked over to take a picture of the river or whatever attraction had caused so many men to gather there. I tried not to think of the families downstream doing laundry.

The line moved slowly. The husband of the lady in front of me had brought napkins from the nearby tamale stand. *Oh no*, I thought. *I don't have any toilet paper.* Luckily, the little baño had a good supply. When I exited, I washed in a sink outside the small room. There were no towels, so I gave my hands a brisk snap to shake off the water.

Once we arrived in Huehue, we transferred to a taxi for a one-hour drive up a steep mountain road with tight switchbacks. It rained heavily and rocks, boulders and mud slid onto the roadway. Wild dogs, water pouring off their backs, waited alongside the highway for a meal of road kill or edible trash.

At last, relieved that we hadn't been buried by a mudslide, we arrived at my friend's house where I met his family. He gave me a tour of their home, showed me my room, and led me to the baño . . . out into the rain, up the steps in the dark to the backyard, across pieces of broken asphalt salvaged from some roadside, and to the little structure of rough boards surrounding a toilet.

"I'm sorry," he said, "We have electricity, but still no bathroom plumbing." A little board covered the seat. Toilet tissue, soaked by the heavy rain, hung from a nail on the wall. He quickly fetched a fresh roll from the house. A crisp plastic shower curtain served as a bathroom door.

After using the facility, I made my way back down to the house where there was running water to wash my hands. I couldn't stay on the stepping stones and my shoes became heavy with thick red mud.

Once in bed, I prayed I wouldn't have to venture back to the lavatory until morning.

I awoke to sunshine. The red mud had begun to dry, and when I reached the baño, I marveled at its beautiful setting at the top of the world, surrounded by fruit trees, vegetables and flowers, overlooking the city of Huehue. Hillsides covered with farms spread out before me like a patchwork quilt.

I got to see a lot on that trip, but I never did remember to pack toilet tissue before going on an outing. Sometimes there was paper, and sometimes not. The baños that didn't supply paper, I decided, didn't have to worry about keeping it stocked or worry about anyone stealing the roll. Those that did supply paper had the added expense of supplying people's pockets in preparation for their next stop. And I noticed that restaurants usually only provided one small, inadequate napkin, or *servilleta*, rather than leaving a stack on the table that would make its way into pockets for the restroom stops.

On that trip I'd learned a lot more about baño etiquette. Here are the rules:

- Always go before you get on the bus;
- Give wet hands a brisk shake to dry;
- Never, never dispose of toilet tissue in the toilet—toss it into the basket or onto the pile in the corner that someone has already started;

- Don't follow a crowd of guys to look at the river;
- Always stuff your pockets with appropriate paper whenever you have a chance.

The bus from Guatemala City to Huehuetenango.

Born Traveler

by
Beth Green

Over the years of my vagabond childhood, my parents and I sailed to 27 different countries. They were my tour guides to life, my five-star cruise ship captains and concierges. They made me a traveler, since even before my birth.

I was conceived in Mexico, born in Oregon, taught my first day of school from correspondence books in a fishing village in Alaska. The tooth fairy left me *pesos*, *dolares* and *bolivares*. I used them to buy ice cream on Mexican beaches. My parents took me on a steam train in Costa Rica, fed me the fruit of the cashew and cocoa, let strangers admire my green eyes and light hair.

My father was the planner. He negotiated our way both in language and trailblazing. He had the chart books, the ideas, the lingo. When I was 8, he let me look through his sextant to determine our position by the sun, and by the time I was 12, I was helping him plot our boat's way across the Pacific Ocean.

My mother was the visualizer. She took my dad's plans and made wherever we ended up our home. She provisioned the boat—who do you know who can plan food for a family of three for three months?—and made our boat seem like a little piece of America even far away. She made sure we kept American family traditions like Christmas and Thanksgiving—even if the Christmas tree was made from green cloth and hung with seashells. And we ate roast chicken instead of turkey.

For 13 years, I was the tourist. I collected foreign coins and postcards. I watched people fishing and swimming on Bahamian islands and longed for a camera. I kept infantile diaries in careful handwriting, detailing the places we traveled, the friends I met. My ears were pierced on Martinique when I was 7. I had a beach *piñata* party in Venezuela when I turned 8. At 9, I watched baby sea turtles hatch and waddle to the waves during a beautiful Puerto Rican dawn. I kissed a boy for the first time at 12 in New Zealand. In Polynesia, I started appreciating pop music. I compiled and illustrated scrapbooks of Fiji and Samoa.

And then, we stopped. I had to start high school. My parents wanted me to attend a real school, in the States.

Correspondence school served us well for the first years, but my parents worried about my future. I could speak passable Spanish, was a whiz at geography, understood the cultural distinction between Maori, Polynesian and Melanesian. I read the complete works of Shakespeare during the lazy days we sailed north, closer to America.

But when we reached Southeast Alaska, ready for me to

begin my freshman year at Juneau-Douglas High School, I learned that all my travels and all my parents' guidance when traveling the Western Hemisphere didn't help me fit in. I had never seen MTV. I couldn't use a computer. I had no "normal" clothes. I had never taken a physical education or music class.

Perhaps hardest, I'd never lived in one place before. After just three months of high school, I was ready to go somewhere else. Winter had set in. I was starting to make friends, but the sameness of seeing unvarying scenery—even the gorgeous mountains of Southeast Alaska—made my teeth chatter with wanderlust.

In retrospect, it was harder for my parents. For years, they'd lived a peripatetic life free from schedules. They lived in sunny climates and had plenty of time to visit their many eclectic friends. Our needs were simple. Now they had to face modern life again, including credit cards and bills. We still lived on the boat, but they needed to buy a car and start my dad's business as a carpenter and contractor. He joined the Chamber of Commerce. We got a phone put in on the boat to take calls from clients. Mom stopped painting tropical flowers and birds and started substitute teaching to supplement his income.

For four years we toiled, but soon enjoyed the life we then were leading. My parents built a house and sold it for a profit. Mom managed to sneak in more painting time and started doing Southeast Alaskan shipwrecks instead of island girls and coral reefs. Dad continued scuba diving, sometimes hunting giant king crab. I took drama, made friends, wrote for the school newspaper, and never, ever, told anyone except my closest friends that I lived on a boat. I wanted to fit in, but deep down I couldn't wait to start traveling again.

Four years finally melted away in the spring of 1998 when I graduated from high school with honors.

I had managed to fulfill my parents' ambition, the reason they cut short their sailing. Now I had prospects, my own course plotted. I was going to college. I knew that after years of trailing my parents, it was finally time for me to become the planner, the visualizer, my own guide.

My mind occupied by plans for college, I was surprised when my parents announced they would go on their own trip before I left. They took a white van, built a plywood frame for a mattress in the back, packed all their camping and fishing gear, and met some old friends for a month-long drive around the interior of Alaska. I felt abandoned. I was the one who should have been leaving. I was the one who was opening wings and ready to fly.

But that itch I could feel through the layers of wool socks in the Alaskan winter—the travel itch—hadn't it sprung from the genes that my parents had given me? Of course, this was their freedom, too. Their duty as parents complete, they were also ready to travel again.

Too soon, the end of summer came. The beautiful Alaskan August days dissolved in drizzle, and my parents came back, only to pack their white van full again, this time with my things. We had time for one last family trip.

We got in the van early one morning and headed for Canada. From there, we drove south to Idaho, where I'd go to college. Dad plotted our route. It would take three days. Mom planned the extras. We would stop when we wanted. We might see wildlife. We could bathe in a hot spring. I sat in the back and talked to them. I tried to take pictures out of the window and collected postcards from gas stations.

It was the best graduation present I could have had. On the road we relaxed, seamlessly, back into our old dynamic. This was how I remembered my childhood, my parents: traveling. We were on a highway, not a boat, but the feeling was the same. We were experiencing life together.

We were truly living.

Top left: Beth and mom inside their boat.

Top right: Beth now lives in Southeast Asia where she teaches English.

Bottom: Beth on the dock with her parents, ready for her freshman high school dance.

NYMB Series Founders

Together, Dahlynn and Ken McKowen have 60-plus years of professional writing, editing, publication, marketing and public relations experience. Full-time authors and travel writers, the two have such a large body of freelance work that when they reached more than 2,000 articles, stories and photographs published, they stopped counting. And the McKowens are well respected ghostwriters, having worked with CEOs and founders of some of the nation's biggest companies. They have even ghostwritten for a former U.S. president and a few California governors and elected officials.

From 1999 to 2009, Ken and Dahlynn were consultants and coauthors for *Chicken Soup for the Soul*, where they collaborated with series founders Jack Canfield and Mark Victor Hansen on several books such as *Chicken Soup for the Entrepreneur's Soul; Chicken Soup for the Soul in Menopause; Chicken Soup for the Fisherman's Soul;* and *Chicken Soup for the Soul: Celebrating Brothers and Sisters.* They also edited and ghost-created many more Chicken titles during their tenure, with Dahlynn reading more than 100,000 story submissions.

For highly acclaimed outdoor publisher Wilderness Press, the McKowens' books include national award-winner *Best of California's Missions, Mansions and Museums; Best of Oregon and Washington's Mansions, Museums and More;* and *The Wine-Oh! Guide to California's Sierra Foothills.*

Under Publishing Syndicate, the couple authored and published *Wine Wherever: In California's Mid-Coast & Inland Region*, and are actively researching wineries for *Wine Wherever: In California's Paso Robles Region*, the second book in the Wine Wherever series.

If that's not enough, the McKowens are also the creators of the Wine Wherever iPhone mobile winery-destination journaling app and are currently creating a travel television show under the same brand (www.WineWherever.com).

Dahlynn and Ken in Saigon, Ken whale watching at Big Sur and Dahlynn calling home from Venice.

NYMB Co-Creator

About Terri Elders

In 1987, Terri Elders ran away from her hometown of Long Beach, California and joined the Peace Corps. She was 50 years old at the time. Terri lived overseas for 10 years in four developing countries: Belize, Guatemala, Dominican Republic and Seychelles.

In 2000, Terri married Ken Wilson. They shared adventures in England, Scotland, Wales, Ireland, Germany, Switzerland, Austria, Estonia, Latvia, Russia, Sweden, Finland, Denmark, Canada, Alaska, Italy, Monaco and Malta.

From 2000 to 2004, Terri—who is a licensed clinical social worker—worked at Peace Corps Headquarters in Washington, D.C., providing technical assistance on community health and HIV/AIDS overseas programs. During her tenure, she visited remote rural areas of many countries, including Ecuador, Mongolia, Honduras, Moldova, Samoa, Guyana, Uzbekistan, Kyrgyz Republic, Ukraine and Thailand.

Now widowed, Terri lives in the country in Northeast Washington with two dogs and three cats. She continues to travel. In 2010 and 2011, she attended the University of Cambridge International Summer School. In the Dickens Bicentennial Year of 2012, Terri celebrated her favorite novelist by attending events honoring him in both Philadelphia and London. In 2013, she'll travel to Oxford University in England to study the history of the English language.

Terri is a public member of the Washington State Medical Quality Assurance Commission and serves on the board of Colville Branch American Association of University Women. In 2003, the UCLA Graduate School of Public Policy and Social Affairs honored her as a Distinguished Alumna. In 2006, Terri received UCLA's Alumni Award for Community Service.

Terri's stories and articles have appeared in dozens of periodicals and anthologies. She's the co-creator for two upcoming *Not Your Mother's Book* titles—*NYMB...On Sharing Secrets* and *NYMB...My First Time*. Terri blogs at http://atouchoftarragon.blogspot.com/

Terri in Oxford, England

Contributor Bios

Diana M. Amadeo, multi-award winning author, sports a bit of pride in having 500 publications with her byline in books, anthologies, magazines, newspapers and online. Yet, she humbly, persistently, tweaks and rewrites her thousand or so rejections with eternal hope that they may yet see the light of day.

Kathleene Baker resides in Plano, Texas, with husband, Jerry, and three fur kids: Hank, Samantha and Abby. She has contributed to many publications, online newsletters, newspapers, *Chicken Soup for the Soul* and writes weekly, monthly and quarterly columns. Kathleene promotes dog rescue with fervor, and is co-creator of *NYMB...On Dogs*.

Al Batt of Hartland, Minnesota is a storyteller and humorist. He is a newspaper columnist, radio and TV personality, gag writer of syndicated cartoons, and columnist for *Bird Watcher's Digest*. Al speaks at festivals, conferences and conventions all over the world. His mother thinks he's special.

Arthur Bowler, a U.S./Swiss citizen and graduate of Harvard Divinity School, is a writer, speaker and minister in English and German. He is currently seeking representation for his book, *A Prayer and a Swear*. Contact www.arthurbowler.ch or bowler@bluewin.ch

Erik Bundy is an award-winning poet and short story writer who lives in the magical North Carolina woods where mice claiming to be cousins move in during winter then take his towels when they leave in spring. The federal government pays him not to work in one of their offices.

Kathe Campbell lives her dream on a Montana mountain with her mammoth donkeys, a Keeshond and a few kitties. Three children, eleven grandkids, and four greats round out the herd. She is a prolific writer on Alzheimer's and a contributing author to the *Chicken Soup for the Soul* series, medical journals and magazines.

David Carkeet has written six comic novels, among them a trilogy featuring linguist-hero Jeremy Cook—*Double Negative, The Full Catastrophe* and *The Error of Our Ways*. His most recent novel is *From Away*, a mystery set in Vermont.

Elynne Chaplik-Aleskow is a Pushcart Prize nominated author and award-winning educator and broadcaster. She is founding general manager of WYCC-TV/PBS and distinguished professor emeritus of Wright College in Chicago. Her stories and essays have been published in numerous anthologies and magazines. Her husband, Richard, is her muse. Visit http://LookAroundMe.blogspot.com

Marlene Chism is a professional speaker, trainer and the author of *Stop Workplace Drama* (Wiley 2011). For more information, visit www.marlenechism.com or www.stopworkplacedrama.com.

Sarah Chrisman was born and raised in a suburb of Seattle. She graduated from the University of Washington in 2002 with two degrees: one in French, the other in International Studies. "Imperial Benediction" relates an event which occurred while she was teaching English in Japan in 2006.

SuzAnne C. Cole is a retired college instructor. Her essays have been published in *Newsweek, Houston Chronicle, San Antonio Express-News, Baltimore Sun* and many anthologies. She and her husband have hiked the world including Nepal, Iceland, China, Peru, Austria, Chile, Australia, Argentina, Panama, New Zealand, Great Britain, Turkey and Russia.

Eldon Dale is a native Californian as is his wife, Janis, and their three daughters. His passion has always been to see the world and especially to take the roads less traveled. He has turned his family into travel adventurers, also.

Janis Dale her husband, Eldon, and their three daughters own and operate the family mobile food concession business Country Fair Cinnamon Rolls. It has allowed them the time to travel during their off season. They all live and work in California.

Pamela Frost lives in Medina, Ohio. Her award winning book, Houses of Cards, (available from Amazon and Kindle) is the story of a family who tried to get rich in real estate and their hilarious misadventures. She is co-creator of *NYMB...On Do-It-Yourselfers* and *NYMB...RV Adventures*, both coming soon.

Eve Gaal's diverse writing is available on Amazon in anthologies, stories, poems and a novel. Read "Loser's Ledge" in *Fiction Noir-13 Stories* or non-fiction in *God Makes Lemonade*. Find humorous non-fiction titled "Life is Good" in *Not Your Mother's Book . . . On Dogs*. More of Eve's writing at http://thedesertrocks.blogspot.com.

Farah Ghuznavi's work has been featured in the U.K., U.S., Canada, Singapore, India, Nepal and her native Bangladesh. "Judgement Day" was highly commended in the 2010 Commonwealth Short Story Competition, and "Getting There" placed second in the Oxford GEF Competition. Farah edited the *Lifelines* anthology published by Zubaan Books. www.farahghuznavi.com

Beth Green is an American freelance writer and English teacher living in Southeast Asia. She grew up on a sailboat and, though now a landlubber, still enjoys a peripatetic life. Beth writes articles and suspense about travel and expatriate life. You can find out more about her at www.bethgreenwrites.com.

Stacey Gustafson has a monthly humor column in the *Pleasanton Patch* called "Are You Kidding Me?" based on her suburban family and everyday life. Her stories have appeared in *Chicken Soup for the Soul: The Magic of Mothers and Daughters* and *Not Your Mother's Book...On Being a Woman*. www.staceygustafson.com

Dena Harris is an author, humorist and speaker. Foreign rights for Dena's third book—*Who Moved My Mouse? A Self-Help Book for Cats*—have sold to seven countries. Her next book—*Does this Color Make My Butt Look Big? A Diet Book for Cats*—will be released in October 2013.

Erika Hoffman is a traveler. Many of her tales come from adventures she's encountered on trips. Often, these stories end up in anthologies like NYMB, *Chicken Soup for the Soul, A Cup of Comfort, Patchwork Path* and others.

Carolyn T. Johnson, a freelance writer from Houston, Texas writes from the heart, the hurt, the heavenly and sometimes the hilarious. Her work can be found in the *Houston Chronicle* and the *Austin American-Statesman* newspapers, as well as *Chicken Soup for the Soul* and various other anthologies and e-zines.

Cliff Johnson spent 30 years in prison—in uniform and administration—and was finally released (retired) in 1995. He enjoys golf, distance running, biking, gardening, metal sculpture and above all else, his wife, Scharre. They live in Crescent City, California, the most beautiful place on earth.

Mary-Lane Kamberg flies out of Kansas City International Airport. She is a professional writer and speaker and the author of *The "I Don't Know How To Cook" Book* and *The I Love To Write Book*, as well as more than 20 books for young readers.

Nancy Davis Kho is a writer in Oakland, California whose work has appeared in the *San Francisco Chronicle, The Morning News, Skirt! Magazine* and TheRumpus.net. She blogs about the years between being hip and breaking a hip at MidlifeMixtape.com.

Nancy Julien Kopp is a Kansan, originally from Chicago. She began writing late in life, but has been published in 13 *Chicken Soup for the Soul* books, other anthologies, ezines, newspapers and magazines. Once a classroom teacher, she now teaches through the written word. Visit her blog at www.writergrannysworld.blogspot.com.

Gregory Lamping lives in Kirkwood, Missouri, with his wife, Mary, and their two dogs, Monkey and Scooter. He has had five stories published in the NYMB series, as well as a story in *Chicken Soup for the Fisherman's Soul*. E-mail: glamping@att.net

Lisa McManus Lange enjoys fishing with her boys—but only as a patient bystander. Previously published with *Not Your Mother's Book,* as well as *Chicken Soup for the Soul*, Lisa lives and writes in Victoria, BC, Canada. Write her at lisamc2010@yahoo.ca or visit her at www.lisamcmanuslange.blogspot.com.

John J. Lesjack is a published freelance writer living in and enjoying the California wine country. He may be reached at Jlesjack@gmail.com.

Jennifer Martin is a retired school administrator and former university professor. She is also an award-winning novelist (*The Huna Warrior: The Magic Begins*), screenwriter (*Breaking Ground for Peace*) and professional speaker.

Todd McGough is a retired school psychologist who has traveled extensively in Latin America. He lives in Nicaragua and teaches English at the University of Leon. Todd also surfs every day and plays jazz and blues guitar.

Laurel (Bernier) McHargue was raised as "Daughter #4" of five girls in Braintree, Massachusetts, where she lived until heading off to Smith College—followed by the United States Military Academy. Her constant quest for adventure landed her in Leadville, Colorado where she lives with her husband and occasionally-home-from-college sons. www.leadvillelaurel.com

Pat Nelson, writer and editor, is co-creator of the upcoming *Not Your Mother's Books: On Parenting, On Grandparenting*, and *On Working for a Living*. She has written newspaper columns, contributed to *Chicken Soup for the Soul* and has written one book, Y*ou—The Credit Union Member.*

Sheree Nielsen, a multi-award winning writer and photographer, writes inspirational essays interweaving family, nature and travel. A Missouri Writer's Guild Member, she's served on Saturday Writers board. Publications: *Missouri Life, AAA Midwest/Southern Traveler, AOL/Patch.com, Abaconian, Eleutheran, Nurturing Paws* anthology, *C.H.A.M.P., Cuivre River Anthologies, Folly Current, Storyteller,* among others. www.shereenielsen.wordpress.com

Risa Nye, from Oakland, California, is the co-editor of the book *Writin' on Empty*. Her articles and essays have appeared in local and national publications, and in several anthologies. She contributes essays on the craft of writing nonfiction to *Hippocampus Magazine*. Her "Ms. Barstool" column appears at Berkeleyside.com. She still travels!

Dellani Oakes has been writing since she was a child. Her first efforts aren't very print worthy, but she treasures the memory of them. She looks at the world from a 33-degree angle, finding humor and absurdity in many situations where others might find only defeat.

Linda O'Connell, an accomplished writer and seasoned teacher, is a positive thinker. She writes from the heart, bares her soul and finds humor in everyday situations. Linda prefers walking barefoot on a beach to wearing fancy shoes in the classroom. http://lindaoconnell. blogspot.com

Nelson O. Ottenhausen, a retired Army officer living in Gulf Breeze, Florida, has six published novels, a book of poetry entitled *Flowers, Love & Other Things*, and a short story featured in *Chicken Soup for the Fisherman's Soul*. www.booksbynelson.com

Kathy Pippig lives in California with her husband and furry family. She's written six novels. Her award-winning poetry and stories have been featured in online publications and traditional hard-copy print such as newspapers, books and magazines. She writes to reach the reader's heart and mind and make a difference.

Frank Ramirez, pastor of the Church of the Brethren in Everett, Pennsylvania, enjoys air travel, especially when paid for by others! He and his wife Jennie share three children and three grandchildren. He loves writing and reading, and as a beekeeper has discovered you draw more flies with honey than flyswatters.

Cappy Hall Rearick is a syndicated newspaper columnist, an award-winning short story writer, and author of six books and five successful columns. Featured by the Erma Bombeck Writers' Workshop as a Humor Writer of the Month, Rearick's humor and short fiction has been read and enjoyed in anthologies throughout the country.

John Reas is a former Army officer and telecommunications project manager. This is his third story in the *Not Your Mother's Book* series, and he is discovering how much he enjoys writing and hopes to continue to do so in the future.

Kayleen Reusser has written nine non-fiction children's books. She writes regularly for newspapers and magazines. She has had several articles published in Chicken Soup books and enjoys speaking to children and adults about the life of an author. Her website is at www. KayleenR.com.

J.D. Riso has spent most of her adult life wandering the world. Her short fiction and travel writing have appeared in numerous publications, and her novel, *Blue*, was published by Murphy's Law Press in 2006. She currently resides in Budapest, Hungary with her husband and her rabbit.

Sioux Roslawski, a third grade teacher for the Ferguson-Florissant School District in St. Louis, Missouri also rescues Golden Retrievers for the charity "Love a Golden." Her daughter and son make her puff up with pride, her granddaughter Riley is the light of her life, and her husband keeps her laughing. http://siouxspage.blogspot.com

Mimi Peel Roughton, a former journalist turned personal essayist, lives in Durham, North Carolina with her second husband, Lucien, an architect, and a fat one-eyed cat named Lucy. Mimi and Lucien have five grown children between them. Mimi is working on a collection of essays called *Passing for Normal, More or Less*.

Joyce Newman Scott worked as a flight attendant while pursuing an acting career. She started college in her mid-50s and studied at the University of Miami and at Florida International University. She has contributed short stories to *Chicken Soup for the Soul* and *Not Your Mother's Book*.

Patrick Sisti spent 42 years as a printing salesman until launching a second career as a successful outdoor travel writer. An avid fly fisherman, he loved exploring the Adirondacks near his home of Indian Lake, New York. In late 2012, Patrick passed away suddenly after a day of canoeing and fishing.

Gia Sola followed a successful career track that started out on Wall Street then veered west to California, where she's carved a new identity as a writer. This story chronicles her adventure in Paris after reconnecting with her "ex" and his new wife. It's a scene stranger than Gia's fiction.

Annmarie B. Tait lives in Conshohocken, Pennsylvania with her husband, Joe Beck, where she enjoys cooking and other crafts. She has contributed to several volumes of *Chicken Soup for the Soul, Reminisce Magazine* and numerous other anthologies. She is a recent nominee for the annual Pushcart Prize literary award. irishbloom@aol.com.

Samantha Ducloux Waltz gives people inspiration, courage and a fresh perspective on life as the writer of more than 50 creative non-fiction stories published in *Chicken Soup for the Soul, A Cup of Comfort* and other anthologies, as well as *Redbook* and *The Christian Science Monitor*. More at www.pathsofthought.com.

Ernie Witham writes the nationally syndicated column "Ernie's World" for the *Montecito Journal* in Santa Barbara, California. He is also the author of two humor books and leads humor writing workshops in several cities. He is on the permanent faculty of the Santa Barbara Writer's Conference.

Story Permissions

Tracking Hurricane Bill © 2011 Diana M. Amadeo
Only in Texas © 2012 Kathleene S. Baker
We Didn't Take Any Pictures © 2001 Allen Edward Batt
Alaska or Bust © 2011 Arthur Wilson Bowler
I'm Ready for My Close-Up © 2013 Erik Bundy
Smack-Dab Middle © 2011 Kathleen M. Campbell
How to Err in Italian © 1999 David Carkeet
My Breakfast at Tiffany's © 2009 Elynne Chaplik-Aleskow
Catching a Cab in NYC © 2008 Marlene Chism
Imperial Benediction © 2008 Sarah A. Chrisman
Always Look a Tiger in the Eye © 2003 SuzAnne C. Cole
Welcome to Cameroon! © 2012 Eldon Dale
A Family Affair © 2012 Janis Dale
Dig a Hole © 2006 Julie Douglas
Craving Creature Comforts © 2011 Theresa J. Elders
Geared up in Guatemala © 2010 Theresa J. Elders
High Stakes on the High Seas © 2012 Pamela Frost
One Night in Paris © 2012 Eve Gaal
Old Delhi, New Tricks © 2011 Farah Ghuznavi
Born Traveler © 2008 Elizabeth Green
Glamour on the Go © 2012 Dena Harris
Rhodes Scholar © 2009 Erika Hoffman
A Bawdy Night at Tahoe © 2008 Carolyn T. Johnson
The Big One © 2004 Cliff Johnson
When Pigs Fly © 2009 Mary-Lane Kamberg
Surrealism Express © 2013 Nancy Davis Kho
There's a Small Hotel © 2011 Nancy J. Kopp
They Only Come Out at Night © 2012 Gregory Lamping
Patience in Princeton, BC © 2012 Lisa Lange
Aloha Spirit Revisited © 2009 John J. Lesjack
Spanglish © 2012 Jennifer N. Martin
Celebrating Saint Somebody © 2011 Todd Douglas McGough
Lounge or Lunge © 2012 Laurel J. McHargue
Priceless © 2013 Dahlynn J. McKowen

Rules of the Road © 2013 Dahlynn J. McKowen
In Search of Satisfaction © 2013 Kenneth D. McKowen
The Potties of Guate © 2008 Patricia A. Nelson
No Bad Juju Allowed © 2010 Sheree K. Nielsen
Sunny Side Up in Panzano © 2012 Risa Nye
Ordering A la Carte © 2012 Linda O'Connell
A Touch of Luck © 2011 Nelson O. Ottenhausen
War in the Skies © 2012 Patch Inc. Used with permission.
Beauty and the Beasts © 2003 Kathy Anne Pippig
Inner Ear, Outer Limits © 2011 Frank Ramirez
International House of Band-Aids © 2006 Cappy Hall Rearick
Murder on the Good Ship Lollipopooza © 2011 Cappy Hall Rearick
Corpus Christi Shrimp Run © 2012 John Reas
Moose Meadows Waterloo © 2006 Kayleen Reusser
Half Right © 2012 Sioux Roslawski
A Faux Pas in Paradise © 2010 Mimi Peel Roughton
We'll Always Have Vectis © 2010 Joyce Newman Scott
Uncle Roy vs. GPS © 2004 Patrick Sisti
The Dark Side of the City of Light © 2010 Gail Sola
The Williamsburg Shuffle © 2012 Annmarie B. Tait
Of Trust and Travel © 2012 Samantha Ducloux Waltz
Creature Feature © 2005 Ernest S. Witham, Jr.
The Island of Bones—But Not Mine © 2005 Ernest S. Witham, Jr.

Photo Permissions

Except as indicated below, the photos in this book were provided by the story contributors and used with their permission.

Page 88 (all photos) provided by Jacqueline Ball
Page 113 provided by Pat Nelson
Page 296 (top right photo) provided by D.C. Pelka
Page 299 (top photo) provided by Kathy Partak

Photos provided by Publishing Syndicate:
Pages xi, 35, 92, 108, 128, 152, 185, 196, 212, 299 (two bottom photos)

Publishing Syndicate

Publishing Syndicate LLC is an independent book publisher based in Northern California. The company has been in business for more than a decade, mainly providing writing, ghostwriting and editing services for major publishers. In 2011, Publishing Syndicate took the next step and expanded into a full-service publishing house.

The company is owned by married couple Dahlynn and Ken McKowen. Dahlynn is the CEO and publisher, and Ken serves as president and managing editor.

Publishing Syndicate's mission is to help writers and authors realize personal success in the publishing industry, and, at the same time, provide an entertaining reading experience for its customers. From hands-on book consultation and their very popular and free monthly *Wow Principles* publishing tips e-newsletter to forging book deals with both new and experienced authors and launching three new anthology series, Publishing Syndicate has created a powerful and enriching environment for those who want to share their writing with the world. (www.PublishingSyndicate.com)

NYMB Needs Your Stories!

We are looking for hip, fun, modern and very-much-today type stories, just like those in this book, for 30 new titles in the *NYMB* series. Published contributors are compensated.

Submission guidelines at www.PublishingSyndicate.com

315